Working Women in South-East Asia

Development, Subordination and Emancipation

NOELEEN HEYZER

Open University Press

Milton Keynes · Philadelphia

Open University Press
Open University Educational Enterprises Limited
12 Cofferidge Close
Stony Stratford
Milton Keynes MK11 1BY, England

and
242 Cherry Street
Philadelphia, PA 19106, USA

First Published 1986

British Library Cataloguing in Publication Data
Heyzer, Noeleen
   Working women in South-East Asia: development,
   subordination and emancipation.
   1. Women—Asia, South-Eastern—Social conditions
   I. Title
   305.4″2″0959   HQ1745.8

   ISBN 0-335-15384-4
   ISBN 0-335-15383-6 Pbk

Library of Congress Cataloging in Publication Data
Main entry under title:
Heyzer, Noeleen.
   Working women.
   1. Women—Asia, South-Eastern—Social conditions.
2. Women—Asia, South-Eastern—Economic conditions.
3. Women—Employment—Asia, South-Eastern.   4. Women's
rights—Asia, South-Eastern.   I. Title.
HQ1745.8.H49   1985   305.4″3   85-28448

ISBN 0-335-15384-4
ISBN 0-335-15383-6 (Pbk)

Text design by Clarke Williams
Typeset by Colset Private Limited, Singapore.
Printed in Great Britain at the Alden Press, Oxford.

In memory of
Ong Choo Lian
&
Augusta Ng

Contents

Preface		v
Introduction		vii
Chapter 1	Women and Development: A Theoretical Overview	1
Chapter 2	Women and Rural Change	11
Chapter 3	Women, Migration and Income Generation	36
Chapter 4	The Trade in Female Sexuality	52
Chapter 5	Women and the Plantation Sector	68
Chapter 6	Women and the Relocation of the Textile Industry	92
Chapter 7	Subordination and Emancipation	113
Chapter 8	Women's Organizations and Mobilization	125
Appendix		136
Bibliography		139
Index		146

PLATES

1. Women planting rice near Jogdjakarta, Indonesia. (Photo: ILO). p.19
2. Winnowing rice in the fields, Bali. (Photo: ILO). p.23
3. Day nursery on Prang Besar rubber plantation, Malaysia. (Photo: ILO). p.84
4. Women selecting germinated seeds on Prang Besar rubber estate, Malaysia. (Photo: ILO). p.86
5. Liquid rubber collected in pails by Chinese rubber tappers, Prang Besar, Malaysia. (Photo: ILO). p.88
6. Work in a plant producing toilet articles and detergent, Thailand. Ninety-five per cent of the workforce are women. (Photo: ILO). p.95
7. Spinning mill, Republic of Korea. (Photo: ILO). p.99

Preface

The book documents and analyses the subordination of women as well as confronts the possibilities and problems of emancipation in South-East Asia, a region undergoing a process of social fermentation and rapid change. In these chapters women are understood not in isolation but as people who are intricately working within the structures, processes and changes found in the various South-East Asian societies. I try to provide convincing accounts of what is happening to women in varied real life situations and to set these in a broader regional context and theoretical framework. The book does not provide quick, easy and magical roads to emancipation but shows some of the attempts and struggles for it.

In a society where the academic tradition is relatively new and people are (healthily) more action-oriented, I am always confronted by the question whether writing about these issues makes any difference. I have not resolved this problem but have felt within myself the pressure to write in order to capture, clarify, reflect and think. This book is an effort at sharing these thoughts and reflections.

Although I bear responsibility for writing the manuscript, the book is, in a sense, the outcome of the interaction between the different groups of working women written about and the community of interested women researchers. I would like to first thank all the working women who participated in the creation of this book. Without their interest this work would have been impossible.

The manuscript has been greatly enriched by the comments received from many people who read the various chapters and from discussions in seminars and workshops at which some of these chapters were presented. I would like to thank, in particular, Kate Young and Manfred Bienefeld for their comments on the informal sector; Ann Stoler, Zubeida Ahmed and Robin Cohen for comments on women plantation workers; Constanza Fernandez for helping in the chapter on prostitution and Teeranat for doing some of the interviewing; Diane Elson, David Wield and Hazel Johnson for comments on the section documenting the women textile workers; Daw Aye and Nancy Vivianne for responding to the section on women and development planning.

Many friends have given me support and encouragement during the preparation of this book. Special mention must go to Janet Lim, Joan Clarke, D. Baljinnyam and Pasuk Phongpaichit.

Finally, I must thank all members of my household, especially Lilianne and Pauline, for understanding why we did not do many things while the book was being written.

Kuala Lumpur
Malaysia

NOELEEN HEYZER

Introduction

During the last decade there has been increasing concern about the position of women in society, the relations between men and women, and among women from different social groups. Within this theme, intellectual debate has focused on two major and concomitant aspects: the subordination and emancipation of women,[1] especially women in poverty groups. These two aspects are pertinent in the context of South-East Asia where societies are undergoing rapid economic, political and cultural change.

Many countries in South-East Asia immediately after the colonial period have expressed a commitment to constructing a 'new' society in which the generation of wealth and the eradication of poverty and inequality would be top priority. This reconstruction necessarily involves the dual processes of the decomposition of certain social arrangements and reconsolidation and establishment of new social relations and structures. These processes have been studied mainly within the paradigm of modernization and development.[2] There have also been attempts to examine these changes from the perspective of the international division of labour and capital accumulation.[3] Important as these dimensions are, they remain incomplete in the understanding of the human situation if they leave out the whole essential dimension of human interaction at the everyday level. This dimension, ultimately, is the social reality within which people create their own patterns of emancipation and, in the process, spearhead changes of social relationships. This is especially true for women. At this level women's work and struggle become highly visible. Women are central to processes of change as much as the maintenance of life. Much of this work is done without pay and through non-market exchange relationships. It remains in the realm of the 'informal' and as such has frequently been overlooked by policy-makers and considered as too 'ordinary' for consideration by social scientists. Yet, many structures of society would collapse if non-market relationships and women's work were withdrawn.

The centrality of women's role in everyday life, ironically, gets intertwined into the fabric of social relations and social structures in ways that create women's subordination and unequal position when compared to men. This is evidenced by traditional marriage and divorce practices, the dowry system, systems of inheritance, unequal legal treatment, women's lack of decision-making powers in public spheres, discriminatory educational and economic practices and differential access to social resources, such as food, new knowledge and skills, status and power, income, land and opportunities. In situations of extreme poverty, women's unequal position is even more pronounced: it is the female child who gets sold or bonded first; it is the female child who first drops out of school and, when there is food shortage, it is the woman and her daughters who eat last. In short, gender, together with class, ethnicity and caste, is a conscious or unconscious organizing principle for the structuring of economic and social situations.

In the context of rapid change some structures are dismantled and possibilities may be created for the emancipation of women. While these possibilities exist, there is nothing in the nature of change itself to ensure the achievement of equality. Even when the process of achieving equality is generated, this may occur unevenly at different levels and different sectors, and for different social groups. Hence the process of subordination and of social emancipation needs careful investigation.

Area of Investigation

This book investigates the mechanisms through which different forms of gender inequality are maintained and reproduced in a range of work situations in South-East Asia, and the attempts and struggles to break the vicious circle and prevent the inter-generational transfer of similar patterns and causes of women's subordination.

In dealing with the themes of women's subordination and emancipation, there exists a widespread belief among many intellectuals and national and international development planners that the source of women's subordination lies in their exclusion from the main economic spheres of production.[4] The solution often suggested for the emancipation of women is the participation of women in the economy. Consequently, the 'integration of women into the development process' has been the central focus of the United Nations and its specialized agencies dealing with women's issues, and of national governments that have become uneasy about women's social position, or conscious that the dismantling of structures of women's subordination may be a key to achieving larger developmental objectives.

Although the 'integrationist' view represents the dominant paradigm for national policy-makers and international planners, it has been convincingly challenged by social scientists concerned with developing a more powerful theoretical analysis of women's social position. Their critique grew out of their study of social history and out of their observations of, and often involvement in, the actual situations of women at grass-root levels. Their studies on women's work and employment patterns clearly indicate that the 'integration of women into development' approach of national policy-makers ignores the fact that women of the working poor have always been drawn into the economy. Even the relatively secluded 'housewives' have been shown to be incorporated into the larger processes of labour and accumulation.[5] What is problematic is not the lack of integration of women into the development process, but the nature of women's integration, the concept of development itself and the strategies put forth at different levels to bring about capital accumulation. All of these have a specific impact on the position of women and on the relationship between men, women and children.

The premise of this book is that the forms and bases of women's subordination are influenced by larger systems that produce inequalities and are embedded in the social positions and the social relationships developed through the interaction of economic processes and dominant socio-cultural systems. Any efforts at emancipation must, therefore, begin with an understanding of general developmental policies, the international division of labour and the forms of organization and the social relationships through which men and women experience themselves and interact in their daily life. The identification of these social processes and structures is essential before efforts at social transformation can generate positive consequences on gender relations and on women's social position and status.

Any attempt to understand the forms and bases of women's subordination must locate different groups of women in the concrete context within which they participate and live. This book is limited to the study of women in poverty groups as it is at this level that human suffering is most pronounced and emancipation from exploitative structures most urgent. It therefore concentrates on women working in the following contexts: in rural subsistence production, in the 'informal' sector, in occupations that rely mainly on female sexuality, in the plantation economy, and in the labour-intensive industries.

My focus is on changes in the position of women in poverty groups as local structures of employment are transformed by international and national forces of development such as agrarian change, urbanization, industrialization and bureaucratization. I argue that these shifts in employment structures result in four sets of problems for these women in the rural and urban areas:

1. The changes are making it less and less feasible for women in rural areas, especially women heads of households, to support themselves and their children by means of agrarian household production alone. There is increased pressure to rely both on agrarian household production and on money incomes for subsistence. There is an added work burden on women. Yet, if women have no opportunity to earn cash, their children's nutrition will suffer as women's income in these households is critical to family survival.

2. Shifts in structures of employment are accompanied by changes in skill requirements and by greater emphasis on formal educational qualifications. The newly created positions of employment do not necessarily absorb all those previously employed. Frequently unemployment results and pressures grow for the displaced population to use skills they already possess by migrating in search of alternative employment. The problem of who migrates is dependent on the nature of male and female participation in the agricultural system, on how this participation has been affected by changes in the rural areas, and on the nature of labour demand in the urban areas. Migration in South-East Asia takes two forms: the male may migrate alone leaving his family in the rural areas, or the female may migrate either alone, if she is young, or with all or part of her family. In both cases, there is a breakdown of traditional family relationships and, consequently, the emergence of new family

structures with new roles for women. The length of the period of separation and the patterns of remittance are important factors in these changes.

3. The third problem involves the forms that urban sector employment take and the nature of limited emancipation through such employment. The issue is whether 'old forms' of subordination are being transformed into 'new forms' of subordination, and to what extent continuities and changes in women's work patterns and reproduction roles are taking place under the impact of urban economic changes.

4. The fourth problem is a cultural – attitudinal one. Cultural factors have some independence from social structures and may be so internalized into the psychology of people that they have a powerful force even after the actual social conditions that helped produce them have changed. The consideration of cultural factors is essential in any attempt to improve the status of women as culture is inextricably linked with interpretations of appropriate behaviour for men and women as well as what it means to be male or female. Culture influences not only men's attitudes towards women but also the attitudes of women towards themselves and towards each other. It is often assumed that under the impact of 'modernization' perceptions of women change, and with it, male – female relationships. However, even in a situation of rapid change, sex roles and perceptions may be one of the slowest to change. 'Modernization' introduces new role possibilities that often cannot be handled by traditional perceptions of women. The stress and conflict frequently produced are borne largely by women.

Notes and References

1. The term 'social subordination' is used in this book as the opposite to the term 'social emancipation'. As applied to women, the term 'social subordination' is taken to mean the confinement of women to certain activities and their exclusion from others, with a lower value placed on the tasks and social position allocated to women. The term also implies a certain control over women through the operation of gender relationships.
2. Norman Jacobs, 1971, *Modernization Without Development: Thailand as an Asian Case Study*, Praeger, New York.
   Harry Benda, 1972, *Continuity and Change in S.E. Asia*, S.E. Asian Studies Monograph, Yale University, New Haven.
   Hans-Dieter Evers (ed.), 1973, *Modernization in S.E. Asia*, Oxford University Press, Singapore.
   Ruth T. McVey, 1978, *Southeast Asian Transition*, Yale University Press, New Haven.
3. Eddy Lee (ed.), 1981, *Export-led Industrialization and Development*, Asian Employment Programme, International Labour Organization, Bangkok.
   Papers from the 1980 Unitar Conference on 'Alternative Development Strategies for Asia'.
   Bill Warren, 1973, 'Imperialisms and Capitalist Industrialization', in *Industrialization in the Third World*, New Left Review, No. 81, Sept – Oct., pp. 3 – 44.
   A. Emmannel, 1972, *Unequal Exchange: A Study of Imperialism of Trade*, Monthly Review Press, New York.
   Samir Amin, 1974, *Accumulation on a World Scale*, Monthly Review Press, New York.
4. E. Boserup, 1971, *Women's Role in Economic Development*, Allen and Unwin, London.
5. B. Rogers, 1980, *The Domestication of Women: Discrimination in Developing Societies*, Kogan Page, London.
   Maria Mies, 1982, *The Lace Makers of Narsapur*, International Labour Office, Zed Press, London.

CHAPTER 1

Women and Development: A Theoretical Overview

The last decade has witnessed the growth of a vast literature on 'Women and Development'. This has led to an increasing awareness of the nature and extent of women's participation in the creation and maintenance of human society. Even in economic and social planning, 'women's issues', once thought of as no more than welfare issues in the narrow sense of the word, have become issues of concern as it is being realized that nations as a whole suffers losses when women are excluded from decision-making, are poorly educated, overworked and in poor health. These losses may express themselves as problems of general economic and social development. Yet, why is it that in the social sciences and in most societies, until recently, obscurity and low value have generally been attached to women's work? The virtual exclusion of women, their lives, work and struggles can be understood, at the theoretical level, from a survey and critique of the dominant perspectives in developmental theory.

Development Theory of the 1950s and 1960s

Essentially, development theory is a body of knowledge evolved to describe and explain the processes of social change. Development theory that dominated this period was mainly from the Anglo-American tradition. Evolved in the 1950s and 1960s, it reacted to social changes taking place after the Second World War. Development had become a slogan of global aspiration and effort. Colonies in many parts of the world, including South-East Asia, were struggling for political independence and were searching for methods to create employment and to ameliorate their material conditions. Reacting to these changes, development studies in the social sciences were concerned with problems of the 'Third World' as the colonies came to be called. The main focus was on problems of poverty. It was believed that the essential difference between the rich and the poor, was technology and industrialization.[1] To the question as to what was the basic cause of poverty came the answer – the lack of power to produce economically. Economic growth was seen as the key to curing poverty.[2]

International agencies were set up to gather and publish information, to prepare development projects and plans for increasing economic growth. Theoretical models were set up by Anglo-American economists and sociologists to guide the former colonies to an 'economic take-off'. This economic take-off was understood in terms of monetized, market society. The paradigms of these social scientists dominated the concept and practice of development during this period. When these models proved imperfect under the test of reality, theories were set up to explain and search for 'obstacles to development'.[3] The traditional method of identifying obstacles to development consisted of examining the history of one or more economically successful countries based on the market economy, noting certain structures that were present at about the time when economic growth was actively under way in these countries (e.g., law and order, widespread literacy, the family, efficient and honest bureaucracy, strong work ethics, etc.) and then construe the absence of one or more of these factors or conditions as obstacles to development.

It was the common belief of developmental studies of this period that if you introduce enough technology and remove the obstacles to economic growth (seen in terms of the attitudes, beliefs and basic personality characteristics of the 'traditional society'), the societies will start growing. The 'path to development' became synonymous with advancement towards some 'models of modern societies' which frequently referred to models of countries like the United States, Europe and Japan.[4]

There has been much criticism of the above theories. The approach embedded in the 'development models' assumes that the world is a homogeneous reality and that these 'models' can be taken out of context and superimposed on another with the same results. The analysis contained in them is simplistic and a historical. Reality is more complex than the thesis would have us believe. There may be several kinds of development which may rival, assist or contradict one another. The approach used by the above theories suppresses and makes inaccessible certain dimensions of the development problem in reality, and problems of 'under-development' and poverty, particularly the relational nature of under-development.

From the perspective of women, there was a fundamental flaw in the concepts, methodology and research focus of these theories. The theories equated the whole spectrum of human productivity with the narrow concept of productivity measured in the monetized terms of a cash-based economy. The concentration only on the monetized economic sectors and cash and market transactions completely repressed, devalued and made invisible, the principal contribution of women to their societies because much of women's work is done without pay and through non-market exchange relationships. Also, by ignoring the economic reality which lies beyond commercial money relations, the theories overlooked the fact that much of the economic growth and factors for 'economic take-off' were based substantially on the non-market work of women which kept societies going and created the social cohesion which permitted the market sector to grow.

In developing countries, most of the production for life's needs takes place outside cash-based economies. The production and resource allocation of these societies is based largely on reciprocity and redistribution. Markets have existed but these are organized along the barter system rather than on systematized cash accumulation and transaction. Hence the focus on money measures of the developmental theories in the

1950s and 1960s made them poor tools for the analysis of the rich reality of the human situation.

In terms of resource allocation, too, these theories failed to address the problems of inequality – how inequality is maintained and with what consequences. Experience in different parts of the world has shown that where general economic growth is not accompanied by fair redistribution, the cost of subordination, discrimination based on social hierarchies of class, ethnicity and caste, and inequality of access and opportunities have fallen unequally on women, particularly those in poverty groups. These factors were excluded from analysis as attempts were made to forge forward with capital accumulation. So even if economic development did occur, women would not necessarily benefit.

Some effect to deal with non-wage work as well as irregular wage employment emerged in the social science literature during the 1970s in the debate on the 'informal' sector.

The Debate on the 'Informal' Sector

The inability of developing countries to generate wage employment, and the rapid and distorted growth of their cities provided the new context for the concern with poverty in the 1970s. Various international agencies in collaboration with academic institutions sent teams of economists to analyse unemployment problems so as to devise strategies to cope with them. The International Labour Office World Employment Programme (ILO – WEP) was particularly active and sponsored some nine country and city missions. The Colombo Mission, completed in 1970, differentiated open and disguised unemployment, while the Kenyan Mission (1972) recognized that in Third World countries where unemployment benefits do not exist, large sections of the population are obliged to earn some income even if intermittently and at low rates of return. They called such people the 'working poor' and used the concept of the 'informal sector' to describe the economic activity undertaken by them.

Since the concept of the informal sector was first introduced, researchers have applied it to a wide diversity of empirical data, which has resulted in complete confusion about what is actually meant by the term. In one interpretation, the formal/informal sector distinction is used, following Keith Hart, to differentiate wage-employment from self-employment,[5] that is, to differentiate between labour that is recruited on a permanent and regular basis for fixed rewards, and labour that is not. This stress on the importance of income-generating activities in the informal sector led to activities which had traditionally been classified as 'under-employment' being regarded as productive and supplying many of the essential services on which city life depends. In another, it is used, following the 1972 Kenyan report, to differentiate between economic enterprises.[6] The informal sector is thereby characterized by small-scale enterprises which rely on indigenous resources, family ownership, and skills acquired outside the school system; while enterprises in the formal sector rely on international resources which are corporately owned and operate on a large scale in markets protected by tariffs, quotas and trade licences. A third usage developed by the World Bank in 1975[7] makes distinctions within the urban labour market. The informal sector is seen as the 'unprotected' labour market as opposed to the formal 'protected' market. The existence of this highly fragmented market was used to explain differential labour absorption. The central thesis is that employment in the formal sector or wage sector is in some sense protected so that the wage level and working conditions are not available to job seekers unless they manage to cross the barriers of entry.

In part, the absence of specific concern for women within those early interpretations of the concept of informal sector is due to the rather general level at which the casual work sector is analysed. Although the importance of the family was recognized by the Kenyan report as an economic institution in the informal sector, there was no attempt to focus on the labour relations within the family, that is, on how family labour is organized and how work tasks are allocated. It was frequently forgotten that what male casual workers – the contract labourers, the village artisans and small traders – have in common is the inability of their income to guarantee subsistence and reproduction. Not only men but women and children have to be put out to work in conditions of poverty and it is usually their combined effort in different types of employment which makes subsistence of the household possible. The exclusion of women is also due to the 'invisible' nature of much of women's work. A large proportion of women's income-generating activities take place within the confines of the household and it is often difficult to separate the household responsibilities directed at members of the family from those directed at the market. Furthermore, the man is traditionally regarded as the head of the household and is automatically assumed to be the breadwinner.

Since the introduction of the formal/informal sector concept its theoretical adequacy has been questioned on a number of grounds: that the dualist framework is descriptive rather than explanatory; that, in emphasizing the parts, the models ignore the complex linkages and dependent relationships between the two sectors and thus cannot capture the overall production and distribution system of the economy. Much of what has been described as informal sector activities were analysed by these critics as petty commodity production (PCP). Such production, it was agreed, exists at the margins of the capitalist mode of production but is nevertheless integrated into it.[8] Unlike the tendency to view the problems of under-employment and casual work in terms of the 'traditional/modern' dichotomy, the shift to PCP was an attempt to conceive of the problem in terms of an interactionist approach in which different modes of production 'adapt to each other, each becoming dependent on the other and each losing its identity and independence to some degree'.[9] The different modes of production referred to in this second approach involve a capitalist sector integrated with the international market and a variety of pre- or non-capitalist modes.

A number of writers have tried to explain, using the interactionist approach, why the small-scale sectors of many Third World countries include most of the desperately poor. What are the causes of their poverty? To what extent is accumulation possible over extended periods for these people? Although the clues to these questions are to some degree historically specific and are dependent on the political and social framework within which the interaction between the different modes of production takes place, the literature provides some general answers.

One set of arguments relates the persistence of the informal sector to the cost of reproduction of labour power. Writers, here, make the case that in societies where under-employment and low income are the dominant trends, the persistence of petty production and distribution ensures the existence of low-cost services and goods.[10] Under conditions of extreme competition, small-scale producers produce inputs for large-scale enterprises at very low prices. It is suggested that the informal sector is the mechanism whereby the upward movement of wages is kept in control in the formal sector of the economy in peripheral countries.[11] Capitalist enterprises are able to enforce acceptance of comparatively low wages by their own labour force because labour's total reproduction costs are subsidized by informal sector activities. The informal sector produces goods and services at very low prices for those employed in the large-scale sectors of the economy, enabling wages in these sectors to be lower than they would otherwise be.

In a somewhat different argument, McGee[12] argues that since family employment predominates in the petty production and distribution sectors, the household unit is forced to absorb the stress created by low wage employment and under-employment and the State is able to cut down on social welfare investment. The implication here is that in some way it is in the State's interest to maintain the petty commodity sector, in a situation when development has failed to create 'modern sector' employment for a substantial proportion of the population.

In essence, the picture that emerges is that in a situation of high surplus labour when demographic growth outpaces economic growth, the extraction of surplus value depends on the creation of a stable structural arrangement that reduces the cost of reproduction of labour for the overall economy. This structural arrangement is the urban informal sector which compensates for concessions made to the organized segments of the working class. In fact, the formal sector is parasitic on the informal sector. The ability of small-scale operators to reduce input costs of goods and services is strongly linked to the large amount of unpaid domestic labour and cheap labour provided by women, children and others in the informal network of kin and friends. The ability of male small-scale producers to sell their products cheaply under competitive conditions requires that women's and children's work within the small-scale enterprise go completely unaccounted for or be given a lesser value in the computation of labour costs, as compared to adult males.

The reasons for this form of women's economic participation as compared to men, however, are left unexplained by the above writers. Reference to competition alone does not tell us why it is that women rather than men are subjected to this inequitable system of valuation, independent of their levels of productivity.

The issue of unequal value given to labour in different sectors of the economy is taken up in another form by writers dealing with the structure of the labour market and patterns of employment. Starting from the position that labour markets in many Third World countries are highly segmented, these writers argue that the labour force is divided into sub-markets with different opportunities with regard to employment conditions and wages.[13] Higher status, better paid jobs are separated from the mass of poorly paid, insecure jobs. Access to these better paid jobs is largely determined by a screening process based on educational qualifications. Besides schooling, the political power of different groups of workers, often embodied in the trade unions, helps to decide who are chosen for particular skills, the rates to be paid for particular skills and the nature of the work task. Workers who are socially and politically weak are pushed into secondary positions. A large proportion of these secondary workers are women.

Perspectives on Women in the Development Process

Many women researchers and social scientists are at present focusing on sexual inequalities in economic, social and political development with the aim of changing the position of women. Much work has been done in directing attention to questions previously ignored, to uncover old biases and to develop theoretical perspectives that take account of women's lives and interests along with those of men.

Writers during the early stages of interest in women's issues examined the effect of economic development programmes on the status of women and argued that women's contribution to production had been ignored. As a consequence of this exclusion, case studies done in various parts of the world have consistently shown that economic programmes have had a negative impact on the economic status of women resulting in increasing income gaps between households in different stratas of village societies, in the relegation of women to economic activities that are less productive and even in the displacement of women from traditional economic activities altogether.[14]

Researchers concerned with women in poverty also focused on women's productive roles. They pointed out that the importance of women's productive roles increases with poverty as the survival of poor households is directly related to the economic activities of women in those households. Time allocation surveys indicated that in poverty groups women tend to work longer hours and have less leisure than men. When these working hours are assigned an economic value, the contribution of poor women and children to household income can be greater than that of men. Even with the long hours spent in production, the extent of women's role in reproduction does not decrease, resulting in a double burden for poor women. Unlike women in the better-off classes, women in poverty groups tend not to trade off between child care and income-generating work. When these women are involved in such work it is their leisure time which is reduced. Hence the condition of women in poverty groups is different from the condition of men in the sense that increasing household burdens and pressures for income tend to change women's and children's but not necessarily men's use of time, and their work burden.[15]

Investigations on women and poverty also revealed a substantial proportion of female-headed households. It was discovered that in the rural areas, inequalities in the delivery of agricultural and technological programmes to women heads of households have reinforced the disadvantaged position of these women.[16] Rural women's access to technical information, training, loans and credit, appropriate work facilities, adequate transportation and markets continue to be restricted. While it is true that female-headed households are not undifferentiated and many are not poor when compared to some male-headed households, female-headed households generally are at a disadvantage in terms of access to wage labour and employment. This is due to several reasons: women are less likely to own land or to have the legal rights to own land, land distribution schemes often grant land to male heads of households only, and women's traditional jobs are often low-paying and of low status, with little opportunity for advancement. Because of these reasons, the agricultural resource base for women is smaller than men's and pressures are set up to seek access to non-agricultural sources of income as well, especially in households where women are the primary economic provider.

Recently, a lot of attention has been focused on the study of women and technology. Technology has been shown to be a potentially powerful force in promoting economic development. However, the positive consequences of technology can be undermined by negative unanticipated effects in the social sphere. The issue of concern is who makes the choices of technology. Normally, those least affected by the choice are those responsible for determining that choice, while those who are forced to live with the technological change have little say in the matter. Much of the literature on women and technology in South-East Asia comes from micro-level case studies, particularly from the Philippines and Indonesia.[17] These studies have shown that new technologies intended to raise productivity may remain only in one sector or group, and programmes addressed to men frequently do not have spin-off benefits to women. Concern has been expressed over labour displacement of women, especially in the poorest rural sector, the increased inequality between the sexes, the introduction of new inequalities and the intensification of old ones.

The impact of migration on the position of women and its impact on the family is another major theme of research in the field of women and development. Unfortunately, no comprehensive and systematic work on migration, both rural–urban and, increasingly, international migration to oil-rich countries, has yet been done in South-East Asia. Scattered evidence exists in the literature, mainly from the Philippines, Malaysia and Thailand.[18] The evidence shows that women's role within the household is affected by migration through changes in authority structure within the family where the male of the household migrates. In cases where young women migrate, the changes in their position occur through factors such as rise in the age of marriage, being able to earn income, and the weakening of social control mechanisms found in the traditional contexts. The hardships confronting these women have also been stressed, such as overwork, difficulty of finding secure employment and housing, as well as low wages.

Much of the existing work on South-East Asian women is descriptive and concentrates on the difficulty that women have in obtaining adequate resources and services. Women tend to be focused as isolated groups. There is a lack of investigation on the consequences of rapid growth and change on women and on gender relationships, on the reaction of women to these changes and on the stresses, conflict and contradictions that occur both at the macro- and micro-levels as the result of these changes. In short, the effects of the dynamics and dilemmas of rapid change on women and their relationships have been little documented.

Another serious gap in the literature concerns the cultural factors affecting the status of women. Yet in the process of learning to be women, women in various South-East Asian societies have internalized and accepted certain social conceptions of women and their position in society. This internalization and socialization has permitted the reproduction of a system based on sexual inequality where women are generally excluded from crucial economic or political activities, and their position as wives and mothers is associated with lower status than the roles of men. Any attempt to change sexual inequalities in the economic, social and political sphere cannot ignore cultural forces that exist in society as these forces have defined women's past and may limit women's possibilities, unless modified. Culturally, the emphasis placed on women's domestic roles has set limits to the avenues by which women's authority and sense of value are achieved.

Equally neglected in the study of South-East Asian women are women's strategies and organization to improve the condition and significance of their lives. While it is true that women, like men, are social beings who work in socially structured ways to achieve their aims, women also have strategies and organizational capacity to improve their structurally weak sphere of influence and power. In situations where, structurally, power, status and authority are with men, women have often worked through subtle inter-personal skills to influence them and in so doing have come into conflict with each other. In situations, commonly households, where power is equally shared by men and women or where women may even have more power than men, women have formed strong co-operative ties with other women, especially female kin, in the household and even sometimes with other women in the community. Given the fact that social structures are seldom so ossified that human intervention can have no impact, how successful have women's actions been in re-shaping their social world and producing more egalitarian structures of human life, especially with their new consciousness about inequality?

The chapters that follow represent a step in the documentation and discussion of issues generally ignored in South-East Asia. In demonstrating the importance of women's lives in the dynamics of South-East Asian development, in analysing the role of economic and political hierarchies in the subordination of women, and in describing how work and success have been culturally defined, this book hopes to promote a better understanding of the social context for attempts to create a future in which women will no longer be subordinated.

Notes and References

1. The Institute of Economic Affairs, 1974, *The Long Debate on Poverty*, London, Second Impression.
2. Simon Smith Kuznets, 1968, *Towards a Theory of Economic Growth*, Norton, New York.
3. Albert O. Hirschman, 1972, 'Obstacles to Development: A Classification and a Quasi-Vanishing Act', in Norman T. Uphoff and Warren F. Ilchman, *The Political Economy of Development*, University of California Press, Berkeley, pp. 55–66.
4. Willard A. Beling and George O. Totten (eds), 1970, *Developing Nations: Quest of a Model*, Van Nostrand Reinbold Company, New York.

5. K. Hart, 1973, 'Informal Income Opportunities and Urban Employment in Ghana', in *Journal of Modern African Studies*, Vol. II.

6. International Labour Office, 1972, *Employment, Incomes and Equality: A Strategy for Increasing Productive Employment in Kenya*, Geneva.

7. D. Mazumdar, 1975, 'The Urban Informal Sector', World Bank Staff Working Paper No. 211, Washington D.C. See also, D. Mazumdar, 1976, 'The Urban Informal Sector', in *World Development*, Vol. 4, pp. 655–79.

8. Caroline Moses, 1978, 'Informal Sector or Petty Commodity Production: Dualism or Dependence in Urban Development?', in *World Development*, Vol. 6, No. 9/10, London. R. Bromley, and C. Gerry (eds), 1979, *Casual Work and Poverty in Third World Cities*, John Wiley and Sons, Chichester.

9. M. Bienefeld, 1975, 'The Informal Sector and Peripheral Capitalism: The Case of Tanzania', in *IDS Bulletin*, Vol. II.

10. A.H. Bose, 1974, *The Informal Sector in the Calcutta Metropolitan Economy*, ILO World Employment Programme, Geneva.
A. Portes, 1978, 'The Informal Sector and the World Economy: Notes on the Structure of Subsidised Labour', in *Down to Basic Reflections on the Basic Needs Debate, IDS Bulletin*, Vol. 9, No. 4., Institute of Development Studies, University of Sussex.

11. A. Portes, 1979, 'Unequal Exchange and the Urban Informal Sector', Chapter III, Unpublished Draft, IDS, Sussex.

12. T.G. McGee, 1979, 'The Poverty Syndrome: Making Out in the S.E. Asian City', in R. Bromley and C. Gerry (eds), op. cit.

13. R. Edwards, 1973, *Labour Market Segmentation*, Lexington Books, Massachusetts.
M. Piore, 1978, 'Dualism in the Labour Market', in *Revue Economique*, No. 1.

14. Irene Tinker and M.B. Bramsen, 1976, *Women and World Development*, Overseas Development Council, Washington, D.C.
Nadia Youssef, 1974, 'Women and Work in Developing Societies', Population Monograph Series No. 15, University of California.
Wellesley Editorial Committee (ed.), 1977, *Women and National Development: The Complexities of Change*, University of Chicago, Chicago.

15. Mayra Buvinic, *et al.*, 1983, *Women and Poverty in the Third World*, Johns Hopkins University Press, London.
Ben White, 1981, 'Population, Involution and Employment in Rural Java', in G. Hansen, *Agriculture and Rural Development in Java*, West View Press, Colorado.
E. Mueller, 1982, 'The Allocation of Women's Time and Its Relationship to Fertility', in R. Ander, *et al.*, (eds), *Women's Roles and Population Trends in the Third World*, ILO, Geneva.

16. Nadia Youssef and C.B. Hetler, 1983, 'Establishing the Economic Condition of Women-headed Households in the Third World: A New Approach', in Mayra Buvinic, *et al.*, (eds) op. cit.
B. Rogers, 1979, *The Domestication of Women: Discrimination in Developing Societies*, St. Martin's Press, New York.

17. Ann Stoler, 1976, 'Rice Harvesting in Kali Loro: A Study of Class and Labour Relations in Rural Java'. Paper presented to the Annual Meeting of the American Anthropological Association.
Roslyn Dauber and Melinda L. Cains, (eds), 1981, *Women and Technological Change in Developing Countries*, Westview Press, U.S.A.
The International Rice Research Institute, 1983, Report of 'Women in Rice Farming Systems', Philippines.

L.J. Unnevehr and M.C. Standford, 1983, 'Technology and the Demand for Women's Labour in Asian Rice Farming', IRRI, Philippines.

18. Udom Kerdpibule, 1984, 'Remittances from International Labour Migration: An Experience in Thailand', Unpublished paper presented to the Workshop on 'Remittances from International Labour Migration', Economic and Social Commission for Asia and the Pacific, Bangkok.

Edita Tan, 1984, 'A Study of Overseas Employment Policy and Remittances: A Case Study of the Philippines', unpublished paper presented to the Workshop on 'Remittances from International Labour Migration', ESCAP, Bangkok.

Noeleen Heyzer, 1982, 'From Rural Subsistence to an Industrial Peripheral Workforce: An Examination of Female Malaysian Migrants and Capital Accumulation in Singapore', in L. Beneria (ed.), *Women and Development*, Praeger, New York.

J. Ariffin, 1980, 'Female Labour Migration to Urban-based Factories in Malaysia', unpublished Paper, University of Malaya.

O. Stark, 1976, 'Rural to Urban Migration and Some Economic Issues: A Review of 1965 – 1975 Period', ILO Working Paper No. 38, Geneva.

CHAPTER 2

Women and Rural Change

Introduction: Some Processes of Development

South-East Asia is a complex region. In trying to interpret current social, political and cultural trends, sociologists are only now beginning to pay adequate attention to the need to understand long-term development processes in South-East Asia. The major question that concerns sociologists is to what extent the period of unprecedented change has brought about a break with the past and how far previous social and cultural formations have continued shaping the social, political, economic and cultural development of the present. What are the relationships between the 'modern' and the 'traditional'? How have development processes restructured South-East Asian societies? What are the present directions and implications of this restructuring? Can these changes increase the prosperity of the poorest strata of these societies?

Given the current state of knowledge, the answers to these questions will be imperfect but some attempts have been made to examine the processes that have shaped and continue to shape the social positions of different groups of men and women in South-East Asian societies. The major processes of social change are agrarian changes, migration and urbanization, bureaucratization and industrialization. This chapter concentrates on the dynamics of rural transformation.

As a result of external forces set up by national and international economic strategies, the rural areas in South-East Asia are experiencing rapid transformation in their technical and social organization. Transformation in technology, the adoption of new varieties of crops, the commercialization of crops, the spread of irrigation systems, have all exerted strong pressures for a closer inter-relationship between the rural and the urban and for changes in rural social organizations and rural institutions, particularly those governing the use of land and labour. Pressures for centralization and greater control by the State, through bureaucracies, are also created by changes in the means of production as more control of inputs, like fertilizers and water supply, is necessary to increase land productivity with the introduction of modern technology.

The focus of this chapter is on the effects of rural transformation on women's position in the rural areas. Transformation in production has not only brought about changes in patterns of production and income distribution but has also resulted, wittingly or unwittingly, in changes in traditional power structures, changes in the use of scarce resources, and changes in the sphere of exchange. How have these changes affected women's work and participation? To what extent are there new roles for rural women as new forms of rural accumulation are being introduced? To what extent are women becoming organized to work together for common goals? An examination of these questions, in specific as well as theoretical terms, essentially means mapping out the changing nature of rural stratification and how it affects rural women.

The Traditional Position of Rural Women in South-East Asia

Women in Rural Households

In South-East Asia, traditionally, the basic unit of the rural farming community is the household and this is the immediate context within which the woman operates. The rural household is responsible for production, consumption and investment activities. Women play an important role in all these activities. In the area of production, they are responsible for carrying out many crop operations, particularly weeding, harvesting, threshing and storage. They are also responsible for small stock, pigs and poultry. When households have access to subsistence plots or gardens women are also responsible for these. The most characteristic feature of rural women is their long and arduous working day. Many case studies of South-East Asian societies show that housework, the fetching of water and fuel, the caring for animals combined with their direct participation in production, occupy the rural women fully, especially if they are from the lowest strata of the rural community.

White[1] on the basis of a sample of rural Javanese households (whose plots of land are too small – less than 1 hectare – to sustain the family, so that the members have to hire themselves out as wage labourers), notes that women of 15 years and over, work an average of 11.1 hours per day relative to 8.7 hours put in by men. Of this time, 5.9 and 7.9 hours per day respectively go into what White terms 'directly productive work', that is, other than firewood collection, child care, food preparation and other domestic chores. In annual terms, the total hours worked (including doing housework) come to 4,056 for women and 3,173 for men.

Quizon and Evenson[2] similarly note, on the basis of a survey of Philippine rural households, that among small farm families men put in an average of 8.50 hours per day and women 8.95 hours per day, while in non-farm families (i.e. those involved in small-scale business and trading not directly linked to agricultural work) men put in 8.77 and women 9.98 hours per day for farmwork plus housework. King[3] whose study relates to the Philippines as well, also finds that women put in more total work time than men do, in both rich and poor rural households.

In a situation of constant poverty the most important struggle is how best to generate and channel available resources to meet nutritional and other household needs. This struggle is made up of two components. The first is the question of increasing opportunities for households to earn income and the second concerns the dynamics of income handling and decisions over the allocation of resources. How men and women operate *vis-à-vis* resources in poor households determines the survival and growth potential of household members, especially children.

The role of women in this struggle is extremely important. Generally in South-East Asia, women in the poorest rural strata not only contribute more time but also generate more income than men within the agricultural household economy. This income is essential to the survival of household members as the men of these households are often employed outside the household at sub-subsistence wages. In regions where there is a high rate of male migration to cities and where remittance is unreliable, this income is indispensible. Many of the women of these households face great hardship as they are responsible for the care of the young as well as the old who are left behind in the villages but at the same time may receive no regular income from their husbands who frequently join the ranks of the urban manual workers.

The importance of women's income to household survival is seen very clearly when placed within the context of malnutrition and under-nutrition. These are grave problems affecting very substantial proportions of the population throughout South-East Asia. It has been estimated by confidential reports of the ASEAN (Association of South-east Asian Nations consisting of Malaysia, Indonesia, the Philippines, Thailand and Singapore) Governmental Consultative Meeting on Food and Nutrition, Manila, 10 – 12 December 1979, that in Indonesia, 10 million people are suffering from protein-energy malnutrition. In addition to this, an estimate of 100,000 pre-school children suffer from nutritional blindness due to deficiency in Vitamin A. Nutritional anaemia affects an estimated 80 per cent of the low income workers, especially pre-school children and mothers. In Thailand, roughly 3 – 4 million pre-school children suffer from protein-energy malnutrition, especially in the rural areas. Vitamin B and Vitamin A deficiency is also a major problem. It has also been estimated that 40 per cent of the adult female population, 30 per cent of the adult male and 30 per cent of the children have nutritional anaemia with the North-East part of the country being the worst affected. Under-nutrition has always been linked to poverty and skewed distribution of food, with families of landless or small-scale farmers, small-scale fishermen, rural labourers, and urban slum-dwellers as high risk groups. In this situation, the role of women becomes extremely important in meeting production and consumption needs.

The dynamics of income handling and decisions over resource allocation vary substantially from context to context and can only be examined in specific detailed contexts. The following account is based on my very brief preliminary case study of the Lampang region in Northern Thailand.

In the village studied, social stratification exists according to the household access to land, cash income and technical inputs. In this rice-growing region, women are engaged side by side with men in rice cultivation, and ownership of land may rest with men and women. In addition, women supplement their household income through vegetable gardening, silk-worm raising, cloth weaving, chicken and/or pig rearing, and petty trading. The annual income of a six-member household in this region is about 17,000 Bahts (22.96 bahts = US$1).

While rice-farming is the principal source of household income, many households are unable to survive on this income alone, and seek other opportunities to increase income levels. Many males are involved as village carpenters, lorry-drivers and manual workers. Many males in the south of Lampang also seasonally migrate to the cities, particularly to Bangkok, during the dry season or when there is crop failure due to irregular climatic conditions. In the majority of households where the husbands have migrated, the women reported that they manage the affairs of the household as well as the farm. In some cases, the adult sons do so. In both cases, consultation frequently takes place with parents, relatives or in-laws, with the woman depending more on her own parents in the absence of the husband.

The husbands usually return to the fields during the period of land preparation, planting, transplanting, harvesting, transporting and storage. During this period, the women work side by side with the men, often with the children and relatives helping. Transplanting and husking are usually female tasks, so also are the raising of pigs and poultry. Tending the cattle is the task of the male child. In vegetable gardening males do land preparation while the women and their daughters do the planting, watering, and transplanting.

Within the village there are some better-off households in the sense that they are in a position to employ others to work their land while their members are involved in shop-keeping, trading and sub-contracting not only in the village but also in the nearby Lampang town. Their women have more time for household work.

Considerable variation exists among these households in the allocation of income for particular tasks. In the better-off households, generally, economic decisions regarding farm credit, the purchase of farm equipment, buying or selling cattle, the choice of crops for cultivation, or buying fertilizers, are taken by the husband, while decisions concerning the purchase of items for the house and the household expenditure are taken by the women. Both husband and wife decide jointly on matters regarding land. Even when there is a pooling of resources between the men and the women, budgeting and arrangement for resource allocation are open to gender dynamics. Men and women bargain with each other over the use of resources and the use of income is one cause of husband–wife conflict. Since the contribution of women in these households is non-monetary and since men are seen as the breadwinners, the power of decision-making is with the men in situations of conflict. Decisions are usually taken in the direction of upward mobility.

In the poorer households, there may not be any income to pool even when pooling is regarded as the ideal state. Women take the responsibility of fulfilling the basic needs of the household, especially of children in terms of food, health care and clothing. The foremost struggle is to allocate sufficient income for food. When husbands fail to earn sufficient income, even for their own survival, it is the women who find new sources of income for them and their children's survival.

In fact, children's nutrition in these households is highly dependent on the mother's ability to earn. In such households, conflicts about income are often the major source of household tension. The struggle is over the allocation of the scarce income. The question of who actually maintains control over the income becomes important. Many women said they tend to hide their money and do not provide accurate information about how much they have. What is clear is that the rural household is not an undifferentiated unit. There are times when male and female interests coincide but this is by no means always the case.

Women in the Rural Community

In South-East Asia, the rural household is not an isolated unit. Instead a number of households are clustered together into groups with a certain degree of interdependence. This interdependence is not only based on kinship but also on locality, thus forming the village community.[4]

Traditionally, rural village communities are relatively self-contained and subsistence-oriented despite the fact that they have varying degrees of market linkage with the urban sector. Within the village itself, there is a strong tendency for transactions to be intertwined in various networks of social relationships. By 'networks' is meant groups of people linked by some sense of common interest, obligation, or dependence of a social, economic or political nature, based on direct personal acquaintance. Village households are usually intertwined in a number of interlocking and overlapping networks, within which there is exchange of goods, services, mutual support and information.

The labour-exchange networks, for example, consist of households which co-operate in performing tasks which need more labour than is available within each household individually. Perhaps the best known of these labour-exchange systems is the *gotong royong* found in Malaysia and Indonesia based on the principle of *tolong menolong* or reciprocity. In Thailand, this arrangement is referred to as *long khaek*. In all these countries, a number of households help each other with the planting, harvesting or threshing of rice or even with tasks such as cooking, child care and house-building. There is an understanding that each participating household will benefit in proportion to the assistance which it makes available to the group. The precise nature of these networks varies from place to place and often includes the provision of food for the workers by each 'host' in turn, and may extend to some form of assistance for member households whose crop fails. Women play central roles in these non-market networks. Their world is a world of relationships with awareness of strong connections between people. These connections make life in the community safer as they give rise to a certain sense of responsibility for one another.

The picture that emerges is that agricultural production is not an isolated part of a woman's life but is strongly related to her reproduction and domestic responsibilities, and interwoven into social networks within the rural community. In other words, for women, farming cannot be dealt with in isolation since it is inter-related tightly to all other aspects of life like child care, nutrition, home-budgeting, handicrafts, water and fuel collection.

Yet despite the importance of women's position within the household and the community, it is the man who assumes the role of main contact point between the household and the larger community. Although women work longer hours, normally it is the men who receive most of the government's training and extension services. When women do have access to non-formal training or advice from extension grants, it is usually in the 'female' areas such as cooking and sewing.

In terms of power relationships, women remain subordinates. Much has been written about the role of patron – client relationship in South-East Asia.[5] The term is used to refer to a dyadic relationship rather than a network, involving people at different social, economic and political levels, and where the nature of the relationship is defined by those differences. In the rural areas of South-East Asia, the hierarchy of power is traditionally based on land ownership. The patron, usually a rich landlord, with his greater access to resources, is able to help his clients gain some access to these resources. In the modern context, as found in North-East Thailand, patrons may be bureaucrats, politicians or simply wealthy men (money-lenders) who are in a position to help their clients or *luk nongs* by giving work, administrative favours, advice, lending money or goods in exchange for labour, rent, loyalty and personal services.

The lack of options and the similarity of employment conditions in other farms often force the agricultural workers to accept the component of subordination that comes with being clients. In other words, there is some kind of a trade-off between the need for security and acceptance of some forms of subordination. Usually the extent of subordination is controlled by the need of patrons to have clients as loyal labourers, and by some traditional custom and obligations which, if broken, would lead to sanctions such as loss of status, gossip or ostracism.

However, patronage is not only an economic relationship. It is also very much a part of the social and political spheres. By providing patronage, the patron establishes his status, prestige and control. There is control over decision-making processes and control over the outcome of the productive process. Within the rural patronage system, women are seldom patrons because of the unequal access to land. Women are structurally relegated to the role of dependants of the clients. As such they usually participate as household workers in agriculture, that is, as helpers of the 'clients' rather than as agricultural workers in their own right.

Even in the parts of South-East Asia where women have access to land through inheritance, the right to land ownership seldom provides the basis for an autonomous area of female agricultural activity nor is the right to land ownership related to women's control over decision-making processes or control over farm production, although the social position and prospects of these women are relatively better than women without the right of land inheritance.

To understand fully the unequal position of women even with the right to land inheritance, we have to turn to cultural and ideological factors for explanation. For example, in Peninsular Malaysia, a Malay rural woman is essentially without status until she is married and has borne children. Within marriage she remains in a subordinate position, although Islam ordains that women should have rights similar to men 'who are a degree above them'.[6] This dominant ideology operates even in the Minangkabau society of Negri Sembilan and the Naning District of Malacca where women, through the operation of the *adat perpateh* (customary law) inherit the rights to the homesteads and rice fields and are vested with the heritage and guardianship of various title deeds.

In practice, women's inheritance constitutes part of the family unit of production, generally managed by men. Because of the influence of the *adat temenggung* (Islamic law) as practised elsewhere in Peninsular Malaysia, there is restriction on women's access to labour supply or male 'clients' when they are the principal managers of their fields as in the case of households headed by women. Consequently women, even with access to land, seldom become successful. Their situation was made worse after colonialism as forest land had to be registered under the name of the men. Women cultivators were pushed completely to the background with the introduction of cash crops like rubber which were planted on forest land.

The Effect of Rural Change on the Position of Women

Agrarian reform is one of the most significant changes occurring in South-East Asia. Throughout South-East Asia, national development plans and strategies have been developed with the support of international agencies to improve the income and welfare of the rural poor. The major rural strategies in South-East Asia aimed at reducing rural poverty have been through increasing the access of the rural poor to land, water supplies, insecticides, fertilizers, credits, and markets, through rural extension services and by the development of new land settlement schemes.

Efforts have been made by many governments to counteract the decreasing returns to labour inputs by increasing the productivity of the land. This is done by investment in irrigation, by increasing land fertility through the use of chemicals and by developing high-yielding varieties (HYV) of crops. During the past two decades, very substantial investments have been made in building up irrigation systems in South-East Asian countries. There have been increases in the percentages of arable and rice areas under irrigation. These increases are usually under-represented by statistics as the expansion of new areas of cultivation outspaces the expansion of irrigated areas. Besides irrigation, there has been a dramatic diffusion of high-yielding varieties of rice, wheat and other seeds, and changes in accessibility of land.[7] The rest of this chapter is concerned with the detailed study of rural change in three countries: the Philippines, Malaysia and Indonesia. What is the nature and the range of impact of rural change on women?

To study the effects of these changes on women's position, a useful starting point is the examination, at the macro-level, of the relative dependence of men and women on agriculture over time. Table 2.1 gives percentages of male and female participation in agriculture from 1950 to 1970. The table shows only sectoral dependence of men and women; a higher percentage does not indicate a greater number. Although problems of defining the workforce may have affected the accuracy of the percentages, in general terms we can say that there have been shifts in sources of livelihood for women and men.

In the Philippines and Burma, women tend to rely less heavily on the agricultural sector than men. A very substantial percentage of women are found in services and in the Philippines in the industrial sector. In the former war torn countries of Vietnam, Kampuchea and Laos, there has been large-scale migration and death of people. Other countries of South-East Asia, such as Thailand and Malaysia, have increased

TABLE 2.1   Labour Force Participation in Agriculture, South-East Asia.
(Male and Female) (percentages)

	1950		1960		1970		1950–1970	
	f	*m*	*f*	*m*	*f*	*m*	*f*	*m*
Burma	64.0	74.7	63.0	72.0	47.6	66.6	− 16.4	− 8.1
Indonesia	78.0	79.0	73.0	75.5	64.9	66.9	− 13.1	− 12.1
Lao Republic	89.0	81.4	88.0	78.7	83.2	75.2	− 5.8	− 6.2
Kampuchea	89.4	79.9	88.4	77.2	84.6	73.8	− 4.8	− 6.1
Malaysia	82.0	62.4	80.5	56.7	68.1	49.8	− 13.9	− 12.6
Philippines	60.2	70.6	43.8	70.1	35.2	62.1	− 25.0	− 8.5
Thailand	88.6	82.9	87.6	80.2	83.8	76.4	− 4.8	− 6.5
Vietnam	85.8	81.3	84.7	78.7	78.3	75.1	− 7.5	− 6.2

SOURCE: Labour Force Estimates, Volume I Asia, ILO, Geneva 1977.

their pace of industrialization and urbanization and this has affected agricultural participation.

Technological Change and its Effect on Women: The Indonesian Example
Throughout South-East Asia, technological changes in rural areas are being introduced as part of government plans and policies. The speed with which the technology is introduced, the rapid rise in profits and the importance placed on linkages external to the village community, may be identified as factors whose inter-action is associated with much of the social consequences that accompany tech-nological change. As the result of quick profits, traditional relationships like the patron – client and the mutual aid networks have given way to relationships that are evaluated in commercial terms. Traditional relationships when evaluated solely from the profit motive are found to be wanting.

With the introduction of technology backed by government support, success, wealth and power are no longer determined largely within the structures of the village society. A characteristic of rural development as pursued in South-East Asia is the 'development' of strong outside agents and support. These 'outside sources of power' may be political, purely economic (private sector), or bureaucratic (administrative extension, input allocation, subsidies). The alliance between the rural elites and the 'outside agents' is sought to guarantee success.[8] Within the village, the co-operative principle of mutual-aid traditions such as *long khaek* and *gotong royong* is undermined as those with enough land and cash income are able to pay for farm help.

A very clear impact of technological inputs into rural areas, whether in the form of irrigation facilities, HYV or fertilizers, has been the increase in the freedom of action of traditional elites or patrons, that is the large farmers, *vis-à-vis* their clients, and the increase in their opportunities to strengthen further their economic and political positions relative to their clients.[9] In other words by relying more on external (urban) sources of economic, political and bureaucratic support, the rural elites or patrons

1. *Women planting rice near Jogdjakarta, Indonesia. (Photo: ILO).*

have managed very rapidly to free themselves from the network of continuing obligations and local distributive systems of the local village.

What are some of the effects of technological change on women? When we consider the multitude of tasks which rural women perform and the limited tools they use in performing these tasks, we would expect that the introduction of technology would bring considerable benefits not only to the woman but also to other members of her family as well. Yet, research that has been done on this area tends to show that the technologies that have been introduced have had negative effects on women from the lowest strata of rural society even if they have managed to improve the well-being of members in the upper and middle strata of these communities.

Some of the best documented changes in women's social position as the result of technological changes come from studies done in Indonesia. Collier *et al.*[10] documented the ways in which large farmers and landlords using HYVs began to limit the number of harvesters, traditionally women, in their fields or to reduce the wages given them. A typical traditional harvest involves women and young girls arriving early in the morning to the rice field which is ready for harvesting. These women use the *ani-ani* (scythe) to cut and bundle as much paddy as possible. As many as 500 to 1,000 women may join in the harvest and a one hectare field can be harvested in one hour. Traditionally, the landowner or patron would permit large numbers of villagers to join in the harvest in order to acquire a share (*bawon*) in the paddy. It shows his concern for the villagers. When the paddy is harvested, each woman carries her bundle to the owners' house where his wife separates the harvested rice according to the local *bawon*, or sharing custom, into two bundles — one for the landlord and one for the harvester.

With the emphasis on profit-making and the breakdown of traditional relationships and obligations, many patrons are seeking to reduce their traditional harvest cost by selling their rice crop before the harvest to a middleman — the *penebas*. This middleman buys an almost mature crop and then arranges to recruit a limited number of labourers to undertake the actual harvest. The *penebas* is usually an entrepeneur associated with harvesting and marketing, and may come from the village itself or from an urban area. By using the *penebas*, only a limited number of harvesters is needed and the total harvesting wage is considerably reduced. The relationship between the *penebas* and the landlord is essentially a commercial transaction and it allows the landlord to break away from the traditional social obligation to open his field to all the harvesters available in the village.

It has been estimated that the harvest cost is reduced very considerably using the middleman. The share for traditional harvesters varies between 10 per cent and 27 per cent in Java. With the use of the middlemen, the number of harvesters is reduced by half and they receive a harvest share of between 7 per cent and 8 per cent. The ability to reduce labour in harvesting is associated with the adoption of the sickle rather than the *ani-ani* as the harvesting knife. More important than restricting the numbers of harvesters is the fact that the *penebas* uses the same persons in each harvest and this severely restricts the number of villagers who benefit from the harvest.

One outcome of this restriction is that more women now participate in the rice harvest as gleaners. Stoler[11] reports that traditionally gleaners were small children and old women from the poorest families, that is, people who cannot keep pace with harvesting work. Now with the pressure of population and an increase in landless families (to which we can add the breakdown of traditional obligations), gleaners comprise a more diverse group of women. Also with the introduction of the HYV which allows a second rice crop, the gleaners can no longer come at their leisure one or two days after the harvest. Now the harvesters are directly followed by men who slash, burn or plough the stalks back into the earth for quick decomposition, or who use the stalks for fodder and garden mulch. In other words, the gleaners must be present immediately after the harvest if they hope to get any paddy. With the presence of harvesters and gleaners at the same time, it is difficult to tell the differences, and gleaners may take paddy that is not a remnant. This has created some tension between the landlord and the villagers. With the introduction of the sickle as the harvesting knife, no paddy is left in the field and the whole gleaning process is eliminated.[12]

The elimination of the gleaning process side by side with the introduction of new harvesting methods, means that women are forced to find other means of survival. In the Kali Loro area of Indonesia, there has been a dramatic increase in the number of women trading who operate with very tiny amounts of capital. Households are forced to survive through a highly flexible division of labour among household members and extreme 'occupational multiplicity'.[13] Each household's income is derived from a variety of sources which constantly change in response to available opportunities according to the season, the state of the market and even the time of day.

It is clear from these accounts that often the various changes, introduced by policies at the macro level, take their greatest toll on women, men and children in the poorest strata of society with women and children suffering disproportionately. Women in these groups face an extremely heavy burden. Besides contributing more time and effort to the household economy and to tasks related to reproduction, they now also belong to households that suffer from increased insecurity and increased dependence on varying sources of income for subsistence as the result of agrarian changes. In other words, they are forced to shape a home based on further reduction of already scarce resources such as limited land and scarce water supplies.

There may be a more flexible sexual division of labour in the sense that the men may remain at home cooking and babysitting to free their wives for trading, matmaking or planting rice. However, this flexibility in the sexual division of labour does not emancipate women in terms of increasing their freedom but is an accommodation made in response to the intensification of pressures for survival.

Similarly, various types of improved technologies such as water pumps and grinding mills have been introduced into the rural areas without noticeably improving the working and living conditions of the women. In fact, it is common to find that these technologies often have negative impact on certain groups of women. One of the most dramatic examples of technological change concerns the decline of hand-pounding in the processing of rice. Traditionally, small rice traders employ a large number of women to hand-pound paddy. However, since a decade ago, hand-pounding was gradually being replaced by the use of small-scale hullers as the dominant technology for rice processing. It has been estimated that on Java alone, more than 50 per cent of the total rice harvest is now milled by hullers. Although this modern technology brings a higher rate of return to the traders than the hand-pounder, the women who rely on hand-pound as additional source of income are adversely affected. The hand-pounding technology was a relatively high-paying job for village women particularly from landless families, many of whom could support themselves through the year from this income.[14] With the elimination of this source of income, these women are forced to seek alternative income-generating activities, often unsuccessfully, in order to subsist.

There is as yet no quantitative estimates of the extent and rate of female labour displacement and what options are available to these women. The present position is that with the current form of technological changes in rural areas, income frequently increases for the upper- and middle-level rural families while there is a tendency for a decline in income and an increase in work burden for women in the lowest strata of rural society. These women have very little access to the technology and the various inputs that accompany that technology (capital, skills, extension sources, etc.).

Also equipment innovation introduced in South-East Asia is usually in the interest of cash crops while the women themselves are primarily responsible for food crops. The latter are grown mainly with the use of traditional technology. This has led to a widening of income gaps and gaps in labour productivity.

Recently work has been done on developing or improving technologies related to crop production and processing, water supply, fuel supply and transportation aimed at improving the position of rural women. Regarding land preparation there are improved hand tools for weeding and fertilizer application that can do the job more speedily than the traditional hand methods, for threshing and winnowing there are hand-operated or pedal machines which are less time-consuming. There are also a variety of new or improved technologies to help with the storage and preservation of surplus food on the farm. All these improved technologies, potentially, can be very beneficial for reducing the work burden of women and improve their well-being and that of their children. However, in reality a number of factors have prevented the benefits from being realized.

Many of these small-scale simple technologies are cheaper than the sophisticated machinery but they are still out of the price range of the women in the lowest strata of rural society in South-East Asia. These women also, because they are poor, have no access to loans or credit facilities. Even when women have access to these technologies, they are given no knowledge of how to operate and maintain the equipment. Consequently, there is a high incidence of such equipment being in storage, being left unrepaired or requiring further investment to maintain. Some of the most striking accounts of this comes from outside South-East Asia. In Bhutan, the small kingdom in the Himalayas, a government official reported how with the advice of foreign experts, sprays for fertilizers and insecticides were introduced to the rural areas. Many of the women had no knowledge about the use of the spray and several of them died through its misuse. Equipment was introduced into the countryside that required the regular supply of electricity which the rural areas did not have. Money was spent installing a power station which required foreign technicians to maintain. In an income-generating scheme for women, weaving machines were introduced.

2. *Winnowing rice in the fields, Bali. (Photo: ILO).*

These machines, however, were too big for the houses of these women. They had to be located in a special building away from their houses. The project was rejected by the women since they had to change the whole pattern of their lives just to accommodate the new technology.

We have sufficient examples now to know if there is to be a positive restructuring of women's social position in the rural areas through the aid of technology, the women must have control over what equipment is purchased, they must be consulted by the technologist at the design stage and their priority needs must be investigated. Already a lot of wastage has occurred in designing technologies that meet low priority needs of women and hence have little chance of being applied while the more urgent problems as experienced by these women remain unsolved.

The Impact of Changes in Access to Land: The Case of Malaysia
Before colonial rule rural production in Malaysia was essentially subsistence oriented and both men and women were granted customary rights to the produce of the land. The colonial administration introduced changes which disrupted the traditional agrarian system.[15] The colonial system of land title registration, the restriction of access to land depending on ownership in the modern sense and the emphasis on paddy and plantation cultivation all had implications on the rural areas and introduced many disadvantages for women.

Traditionally, a family which clears new land and farms it has the right to occupy the land. The heir to the land is the child living and working on the land. In Malay society this is often one of the daughters. This system worked because land was in surplus. Women's work on the land gave them as much right to the land as men. With the introduction of legal ownership, land became a saleable commodity and the motive of accumulation was introduced. The rural economy where land was used only for subsistence was replaced by a system which granted rights to the land and its produce. People who for one reason or another were excluded from this privilege also lost their customary rights to the produce of the land. Conditions were set up for wage labour as the new landlords, including plantation producers, could now establish contractual arrangements with the available labour.

The access to land and the role of land changed dramatically.[16] There was a small group of rural people who, through savings or inheritance, could achieve socio-economic mobility through the accumulation of land. However, the number is small. The groups that benefited most were the urban government bureaucrats and wealthy businessmen.

With the competition from commercial agriculture and the opening up of plantations, the surplus of land was quickly exhausted. Under this new situation, women are overlooked and ignored in favour of men. It is assumed that since the woman farms land as part of a family, she will not be at disadvantage if the land belongs to her husband. The colonial state assumed that the male is head of the household and it was usually the man who was sought out by state bureaucracy and administration. The registration of land was in the man's name.

Even since colonial rule, while land settlement schemes have been set up to reduce rural unemployment and to satisfy the desire for land-ownership, men, who dominate the politics and government of the country, continue to discriminate against women. Although the emphasis is on the full utilization of family labour, i.e. women and children, the selection of people to the scheme is based on the characteristics of the male head of household. Women do not enter the picture.

The existence of land hunger in the rice-growing areas of Kedah and other areas is not caused just by population pressures. Vast acreages of suitable land are still uncultivated. However, the opening of this land for cultivation and settlement is strictly the monopoly of the state through its agencies like the Federal Land Development Authority (FELDA) and the Federal Land Consolidation and Rehabilitation Authority (FELCRA). The slowness of these authorities in opening up land limits the range of choices to the rural poor who have often resorted to illegally occupying the rural land or migrating to urban areas to seek jobs.

The rapid rise in the value of land caused by the penetration of urban interest into the rural areas and by the Green Revolution has led to increases in rent for land and housing.[17] This has displaced many rural poor, many of whom migrate to urban centres. Traditionally it is the men who migrate. It is only with industrialization that young Malay women are leaving the rural areas. What this means is that when the rural sector undergoes changes, men's jobs undergo diversification as it is the men who first take part in work outside the traditional sector, while women remain concentrated in family farming at unpaid or low wages. Women are required to maintain family farms and provide food for the household.

In the situation of labour surplus women's reproductive and unpaid roles intensify while her productive role decreases. A woman's reproductive role reduces her competitiveness with the man in the hiring out of her labour. Since men refuse to share some of this role, it is easier to keep the women within the house while the men 'go out to work'.

Effects of Changes in Production Methods: The Case of the Philippines

In the Philippines, unusually, there are slightly more men than women in the rural areas. A higher proportion of females than males concentrate in the urban service sector and in industry. Prior to the changes in rice cultivation of the last decade, rice-growing was not very labour-intensive. In the mid-1960s short-statured, fertilizer-responsive modern varieties (MVs) were introduced by the International Rice Research Institute (IRRI) and national research programmes.[18] They have been widely adopted by farmers in irrigated and favourable rain-fed environments because their yield is greatest where water management is good.

MVs generally require more labour than traditional varieties because they require more weeding (due to increased fertilizer use) and the increased yields require more harvest and post-harvest labour. Barker and Herdt[19] reviewed 20 village studies of labour use both before and after MV adoption throughout Asia and found that in 13 cases labour use increased, and in another 3 cases remained unchanged. Increased labour has generally been used in women's tasks: intensification of crop establishment (transplanting in straight rows) and crop care (weeding and fertilizing), and harvesting and processing the additional yield. Furthermore, the increased irrigation and shorter-duration varieties lead to increased cropping intensity and more regular demand for labour throughout the year. As the increase in labour demand is principally for women's tasks, new technology has expanded their employment opportunities.

The adoption of MVs has also been accompanied by increased use of hired labour. In a review of 21 studies of hired labour use after MV adoption, Barker and Herdt found an increase in 16 cases. Not only are the seasonal demands for increased labour-use met through hiring in, but family labour also declined absolutely. In particular, women in farm households shift to more lucrative marketing or sideline activities and provide supervision rather than labour in farm production. Thus, the adoption of MVs not only increases total labour demand, but increases hired labour demand, which should benefit women in landless households. More studies need to be made before this trend can be generalized for the whole country.

Bureaucracies and Women's Participation: The Cases of Malaysia and Indonesia

Rural development in South-East Asia as managed by the state is highly administrative in nature, with the creation of bureaucracies both at the national and local levels. Government policies relating to rural development, whether these be land resettlement schemes, the dissemination of new technologies or the delivery of services, are translated into action through bureaucracies. These bureaucracies are given crucial roles in policy formulation and implementation with the government (and international agencies) providing huge overhead capital.

In Malaysia, for example, one of the major aims of development has been to reduce the incidence of rural poverty and numerous bureaucracies and agrarian organizations have been created with the objective of helping the rural poor. Major examples include the Council for Indigenous People (MARA), the Rural Industrial Development Authority (RIDA), the Federal Agricultural Marketing Authority (FAMA), and the Federal Land Development Authority (FELDA). The Ministry of Agriculture alone has 13 such agencies which have activities varying from agricultural research to community development. Such organizations have not only scarce skilled personnel but also a significant portion of the budget for the agrarian sector.

While the rationale for setting up these bureaucratic organizations is to provide the mechanisms for helping rural people, the politics of participation in these organizations determines the opportunities that they make available. The decisions within the bureaucracies are made by people who are removed or isolated from the local reality and implemented through structures that are more responsive to central direction than to the needs of the poor, often transcending the objections for which they were created.

Many bureaucracies involved with development have now taken over the rhetoric of 'participation in development'. However, there is little attempt to move away from 'top-down planning'. The word 'participation' usually only means that people defined as 'targets of development' should comply with bureaucratic innovatives, that is, they should not provide 'obstacles to development plans' which usually ignore the interests of rural women. In effect, bureaucracies put a constraint on the way people act and interact and suggest the manner in which people should be incorporated into the development process.[20] With the bureaucratization process, the confinement of rural women to the private and micro-level spheres of life is intensified. Entry into these bureaucracies is based on educational titles, traditional titles, connections, wealth – resources that poor rural women do not have.

Because bureaucratic structures are traditionally male-dominated and their expansion has strengthened overall male dominance, there have been attempts by governments to create women's organizations in rural areas due to pressures created during the Women's Decade. In Malaysia, at the national level, the National Advisory Council on the Integration of Women in Development (NACIWID) was set up in 1976.[21] This Council does not have a budget of its own and it consists of urban women. Hence, it is doubtful whether the needs and wants of the rural women themselves will make their way up the bureaucratic channels of the Council. Government attempts to reach women in rural communities in Malaysia are carried out through the women's section of the Community Development Programmes of KEMAS (Community Development Division of the Ministry of National and Rural Development), the Ministry of Culture, Youth and Sports and agencies like RISDA (Rubber Industry Smallholders' Development Authority), FELDA, the Department of Agriculture and the Farmers' Organization Authority (FOA).

KEMAS has concentrated on classes in literacy, handicrafts, pre-school centres and family development classes which include home economics, nutrition, and health education. They have also established rural libraries. The Department of Agriculture provides extension services to farmers. Initially their programmes for women concentrated on home economics, but now attempts have been made to shift emphasis towards technical training. There are female extension workers who work with female farmers as well as supervise all 'special programmes' for women. The programmes for women centre around family development and are carried out through formal courses and training workshops. Women are given training in home economics and classes in sewing, nutrition and handicraft. The leadership of these organizations is taken by rural elite women, i.e., the wives of village headmen, closely associated with government administration. The organizations aim to provide rural women with 'education for development'. They conduct classes in cooking, child welfare, sewing, mothercraft and also raise funds for local projects and scholarships.

Besides these women's organizations, young women are found in the youth organizations that have been sponsored directly or indirectly by the Ministry of Culture, Youth and Sports. According to statistics from this Ministry, there are about 4,000 such youth organizations with membership of about 600,000 of whom roughly one-third are women. About 80 per cent of these clubs exist in the rural areas. The activities of these clubs revolve around education, economic and cultural activities. In the field of education, much effort is made in promoting kindergartens where young women members volunteer their time as teachers. Evening classes are also organized for members. The government provides leadership and vocational training for young people in these clubs, often through the co-sponsorship of UN agencies. Within these youth clubs, women members do not appear to take a leading role. Frequently males and females assist in local functions in separate groups.

RISDA, the organization which monitors day-to-day developments in the smallholder rubber cultivations, started programmes for women in 1978. The *Persatuan Wanita Pekebun Kecil* (Organization for Women Rubber Smallholders) carries out activities in cooking, food-processing, serving, income-generation and the establishment of kindergartens.[22] No project in the field of rubber cultivation, processing or marketing has been initiated. There is no intention to exclude women in these activities. In theory any person who wishes to participate in these activities is free to do so. But in practice, the timing and place of training are not convenient for women. Also, as mostly men attend training sessions when they are organized, women for cultural reasons do not participate.

The bureaucratic understanding of what should make up a 'women's programme' seems to be a rigid one which concentrates on women's domestic and reproductive roles. Yet traditionally, rural women in Malaysia have been active in other spheres though they remain excluded from the wider decision-making structures and processes. For example, it was as early as the 1930s that the first Malaysian Women's Movement was established. Their objective was certainly not a domestic one. The founders of this 'Conscious Women's Movement' (AWAS) included many rural women and they were involved in the anti-colonial struggle. Equally in recent years many rural women have not restricted their activities to the household but are actively involved in political organizations.

Within villages there are women's sections of political parties such as the *Wanita UMNO* (Women's Section of the United Malay National Organization) and the *Dewan Muslimat* (Women's Section of the Pan-Malayan Islamic Party). The participation of rural women in these political associations does not, however, represent a changed attitude towards the role of women. The Women's Sections of political parties assume a position parallel to that of women within traditional society. The Section is subordinate to the largely male-dominated party. The Women's Section is seen as mainly supportive. It has yet to become an organization where women push their issues to be included in mainstream development.

There are also a number of co-operative and credit societies initiated by rural women. In Malaysia, women find different uses for credit from men and their credit co-operatives are multi-purpose. Those differences reflect men's and women's different relationships to land and the different decisions that women take in the allocation of household resources. To be in the same credit co-operative with men would mean being subject to competition with men's criteria for the availability of credit.

Trends seen in Malaysia are generally true in many other countries of South-East Asia. In Indonesia, the Philippines and Thailand, side by side with the growth of bureaucracies, there has been a proliferation of rural community development organizations including rural women's associations. Many of these organizations have been created through the efforts of governments in the attempt to induce community participation in the rural areas. Some have been the efforts of non-governmental organizations, voluntary agencies and missionary groups. Although the aim of these organizations is participation of rural people, the achievement of this has proved elusive. In general, these organizations meet infrequently, the office holders push themselves into power. Frequently, the same group of people hold office in several organizations. Members of the local elite or their wives may use these organizations to obtain benefits for themselves.

It has been documented in Central Java, for example, that there is resistance to the sharing of formal power between men and women even at the local bureaucratic level. Women were denied a direct role in establishing and managing the curative aspects of village health organizations. The village men would not allow women to participate in decision-making in the organization. The male-dominated bureaucracy decided that women's activities would be restricted to nutrition which the men saw as separate from their domain – health care. For the villagers the male health cadres equipped with some medical knowledge and a medical kit had a more important and prestigious role than the women with their nutritional kit. The men also blocked the participation of women school teachers who could have provided much leadership for the success of these organizations. There were also rivalries among the women themselves.[23]

Another case study of two Indonesian villages – Pondok Jagung and Rawabuntu, in West Java – found that while there was a 'government instruction' that 'the wives of village heads and other village functionaries have the right and the responsibility to become leaders of the women's community in their territories', in practice the women's organization of the Department of Interior, *Pertiwi*, 'constitutionally appoints the *lurahs*' (village headmen) wives as chairwomen of organizations at the village level. Congruently, the *lurahs*' wives have to comply with instructions from above'.[24] Besides the wives of bureaucrats, another category of women are traditionally looked upon as leaders. They are school teachers, religious teachers, *dukun* (traditional healers), midwives, old women with much experience. While the wives of village headmen are appointed leaders, the rural women themselves have their own 'informal' leaders consisting of the second category of women.

Generally, in South-East Asia, while bureaucracies define problems, shape proposals for the solution of these problems and have access to massive resources, they fail to provide the people they plan for with a sense of meaningful participation in decisions important to their lives. Frequently the efforts of these bureaucracies fail to reach the lowest strata of rural society and have done little in changing the distributions of power and wealth. Usually these bureaucracies have strengthened further the power and economic positions of urban and rural elites.[24]

In their explicit objectives, many bureaucracies enter the rural areas in order to disseminate information on new crops, new strains and the most recent techniques of agriculture and livestock rearing. However, with the spread of these bureaucracies, civil servants and other urban interests begin to extend their influence into the rural areas, often buying rural land as investment, introducing the search for quick profits, the creation of external sources of power for rural elites, and the devaluation of traditional rural relationships and organizational structures. All of these have negative consequences for rural women.

Social Consequences of Large-Scale Rural Developments for Rural Women: The Case of Sarawak, East Malaysia

The link between the position of women and the social consequences of large-scale rural development projects is an important issue for investigation. One development project that has brought about drastic alterations in the physical and social environments and in the life-style of rural people, especially women, is the development of hydro-electric dams.

The development of the Ai Batang and the proposed Palagus/Bakun hydro-electric dams in Sarawak, East Malaysia involves the uprooting and resettlement of various tribal groups, the largest group being the Ibans. Traditionally, the Ibans are shifting cultivators, growing rice as their main crop. The cultivation of rice through shifting cultivation is not only an economic activity for the Ibans but is also a way of life integrated with their world view, culture and emotions. The Ibans also earn cash income from the collecting and gathering of jungle produce like rattan, damar, garu and jelutong. The Ibans live in longhouses scattered along the banks of the Rajang, Balui and Ai Batang rivers and their tributaries. Each longhouse has its own headman and is composed of several *bileks* (households).

Land is commercially owned by the *bilek*. The ownership of land is established by the felling of primary forest. Once an area is cleared, it becomes the general property of the *bilek* and is inherited in the same way as other valuables. Right of access is confined only to members of the *bilek* with women and men having the same access, through the operation of the Iban customary law or *tusun tunggu*. The traditional access to land has changed over time. The Sarawak Land Code recognises the ownership of land acquired by felling of the forest only prior to 1st January 1958. After this date, ownership through this method is only allowed if permission to clear the forest has been given by the District Office.

The most drastic change in the life-style of the Ibans has occurred with the harnessing of Sarawak's rivers for hydro-electric power. Decisions concerning the development of these dams are made by interested economic and political forces, many of which are international in scope. The Sarawak Electricity Corporation (SESCO), with the advice of international hydro-electric consultants and companies such as the German Agency for Technical Co-operation Ltd., and Sama Consortium, are carrying out feasibility studies for two dams – the Pelagus and Bakun projects. SESCO, with the Australian Snowy Mountains Engineering Corporation, completed the construction of the Ai Batang Dam in 1981. The energy generated from these dams will be used not only for Sarawak's needs but also for export to Sabah, Peninsular Malaysia and, eventually, with the development of two more dams and of undersea cables, to the whole ASEAN region.

The implementation of the Pelagus and Bakun hydro-electric projects means changing the whole character of the whole upper Rajang catchment area. About 83 per cent of the population of the area above Pelagus Rapid would be relocated, resulting in the disruption of their existing social, economic and cultural life. A high percentage of very good agricultural land along the river valleys of the Rajang and Balui rivers and their tributaries would be flooded, including areas covered with cash crops like cocoa, pepper, and coffee, and 70 per cent of the paddy fields.

Nationally, the development of the dams is viewed as a way of generating vast amount of cheap electricity to feed new urban centres and industries, not only in Sarawak but eventually also in the neighbouring countries as a way of earning foreign exchange. The Ibans who have been relocated are regarded as people who are ekeing out a precarious existence as shifting cultivators. With resettlement, assigning each *bilek* with a plot of land growing mainly cash crops, it is hoped that the Ibans would change from being inaccessible shifting cultivators to stablized cash-crop cultivators, within easy reach of government bureaucracies.

When the Ai Batang dam was completed recently, a total of 21 longhouses in the upper Ai Batang and Sungei Engkau were resettled in two phases – ten longhouses in August 1982 and eleven in October 1984. More resettlement will occur in the future. Compensation ranging from M$10,000 to M$100,000 (US$1 = M$2.50) was paid. Longhouses were built by the Housing Development Commission and sold to the people for M$27,000 per *bilek* (Phase I) and for M$15,000 – M$25,000 per *bilek* (Phase II). The Sarawak Consolidation and Rehabilitation Authority (SALCRA) was given the task of developing a settled population, living in an accessible manner, exposed to government schools, clinics and rural bureaucracies. Each *bilek* was allocated 11 plantable acres of land (5 for rubber, 3 for cocoa, 2 for paddy and 1 for vegetable gardening). Land is registered and is at present held communally. However, as the crops mature, titles will eventually be given to the male heads of households. The cocoa and rubber plots are managed like estates by SALCRA while the Iban farmers contribute M$60 a month towards the cost of agricultural inputs like fertilizers, pesticides and infrastructure.

The development of the hydro-electric dam and the resettlement of the Iban society have had many social consequences which inevitably affect the position of women. Traditionally, Iban women do not merely undertake cooking, child care, mat-making, basket-making, weaving and general household work but are also farmers. Women frequently participate in rice-farming especially in clearing, sowing, weeding and harvesting. A study of the Iban women's role in Samu on the Paku River in 1971 sponsored by the Sarawak Museum indicated that women are consulted by men not only in matters of the *bilek* and the family but also on matters of the longhouse. In fact, the Iban word for woman 'indu' means not only woman but also 'source', 'origin' and, in harvesting, 'pace-setter'.

With the flooding of their land and resettlement, the traditionally mobile Ibans have been subject to massive changes over which they have little control. They have to learn another mode of living in order to accommodate themselves to a very different physical and social environment – an environment which reduces their traditional mobility, increases their dependence on cash income and changes their spending patterns. The complete change of physical, economic, emotional and psychological aspects of life has produced social stress and anxiety. The Iban's history, oral tradition, singing, dancing and life's experiences are very closely linked with the river, the shifting cultivation of rice and closeness to the forest. Being uprooted from this and resettled on plantations as cash-croppers means adapting to a more sedentary way of life and the need to learn new roles in a new way of life – roles in which often they do not know the cues. They continue to work with remnants of their old ideas and values, combined with an imperfect understanding of the new environment. Under situations of stress and uncertainty, women become the repositories of 'stability' and there is resistance to them taking on new roles that even the men do not understand.

The pressure to be restricted to the *bilek* is reinforced organizationally. Living in 'administered communities' means living within a network of interlocking bureaucracies through which many decisions are made that affect the daily life and long-term plans of the Ibans and over which they have little control. The bureaucratic network decides the wages of the workers, the prices of the cash crops and the method of loan repayment. It is only within the limits of this rigidly planned and highly technical environment that the Ibans can decide their own lives and experiment with social arrangements. The management of the bureaucracies are male-dominated and fail to take account of women's concerns and role in their decision-making process. Women have lost their traditional right to communal land.

The increased reliance on cash income and changes in land use has serious implications for nutrition and health. During my field visit to a longhouse in the resettlement scheme in the Ai Batang area, it was learned that the compensation money was in fact the first time that many Ibans had been exposed to huge sums of money, to the concept of investment, banking, etc. In fact, many were cheated out of their money. Many others spent it on prestigious items of urban living which could only be obtained with money at urban shops, such as hi-fi sets, ovens, Western clothings.

Initially, with compensation, cash is not a problem for many families. However, during the first few years after resettlement they have virtually no cash income from agricultural produce. Rubber matures in 6 to 7 years' time and cocoa similarly becomes ready for harvesting after 2 to 3 years. When the resettlement is not well-timed people miss the planting period for paddy cultivation, and scarcity of food results. Women are forced to turn to their traditional skills of weaving, mat-making and basket-making to meet survival needs.

It has been documented that in Sibu where there is a limited number of employment opportunities for women, 'the largest single category of Iban women are bar-girls or prostitutes.'[25] Given the future development of the lake as a holiday resort and a tourist area which could cater mainly to foreign timber men, coupled with the increased need to earn cash income, there is a possibility that Iban culture and Iban women may become dependent on foreign tourism and the trade in female sexuality.

Conclusion

The impact of rural change on women's position is an important area of concern. There is enough evidence to show that national situations differ too greatly for there to be only one conclusion for South-East Asia. Nevertheless, the examination of some 'before' and 'after' situations has helped in building up information to show that women's status in the household and community is affected negatively by many of these changes. Landless women tend to have fewer work opportunities while women in landed families face more intensive farm work. Unequal land inheritance has weakened women's access to credit and to recognition as farmers in their own right. National approaches to rural women's participation have centred on home economics. The question remains: What kind of organization and training can assist women to take advantage of new economic activities to advance their status? So far bureaucracies and organizations created for rural women have not been very successful in building on the strengths and perceptions of rural women themselves. Their concerns are too narrow and fail to reflect the realities facing rural women. In terms of the future, unless there is an immediate structural change in the labour market, technology, access to land, effective rural organizations for women, and cultural changes in the perceptions of women's role and work, women will be left behind in terms of remunerated work and productivity. This will be one of the greatest constraints to their emancipation.

Notes and References

1. Benjamin White, 1976, 'Population, Involution and Employment in Rural Java', in Gary E. Hansen (ed.), *Agricultural Development in Indonesia*, Cornell University Press.
2. E.K. Quizon and R.E. Evenson, 1978, 'Time Allocation and Home Production in Philippine Rural Household', Yale University.
3. Elizabeth King, 1976, 'Time Allocation in Philippine Rural Household', Institute of Economic Development and Research, School of Economics, University of the Philippines.
4. Y. Hayami and M. Kikuchi, 1981, *Asian Village Economy at the Crossroads*, University of Tokyo Press, Tokyo.
5. Siamvalla, A., 'An Economic Theory of Patron–Client Relationships with Some Examples from Thailand'. Unpublished paper, Thai European Seminar on 'Social Changes in Contemporary Thailand', University of Amsterdam.
   Jan Breman, 1974, *Patronage and Exploitation*, University of California Press, Berkeley.
6. Abdullah Malim Baginda, 1978, 'A Case Study of the Role of Malaysian Rural Women in Community Life', Unpublished paper presented to the Expert Group Meeting on the 'Development of Women's Organizations in Rural Areas', Economic and Social Commission for Asia and the Pacific (ESCAP), Bangkok.
7. William Collier, 1974, Suentoro, Gunawan and Mokali, 'Agricultural Technology and Institutional Change in Java', in *Food Research Institute Studies*, Vol. 13, No. 2, March, pp. 106–120.
   William Collier, 1981, 'Agricultural Evolution in Java', in Gary E. Hansen (ed.), *Agricultural and Rural Development in Indonesia*, Westview Press, Colorado.
   Suehiro, A., 1981, 'Land Reform in Thailand', in *Developing Economies*, Tokyo, Vol. 19, No. 4, pp. 314–47.
   Hansen, G.E. (ed.), 1981, *Agricultural and Rural Development in Indonesia*, Westview Press, Boulder, Colorado.
   Aguilar, F., 1981, *Landlessness and Hired Labour in Philippines Rice Farm*, Swansea University, College of Swansea, Centre for Development Studies, Monograph No. 14.
   Y. Hayami and M. Kikuchi, op. cit.
8. James Scott, 1972, 'The Erosion of Patron–Client Bonds and Social Change in Rural Southeast Asia', in *Journal of Asian Studies*, Vol. 32, No. 1, November, pp. 5–37.
   Margo Lyon, 1970, *The Basis of Conflict in Rural Java*, Centre for South and S.E. Asian Studies, University of California, Berkeley.
   Scott, J.C. and B. Kerkvliet, 1973, 'The Politics of Survival: Peasant Response to "Progress" in S.E. Asia', in *Journal of S.E. Asian Studies*, 4, pp. 241–68.

Scott, J.C., 1976 *The Moral Economy of the Peasant*, Yale University Press, New Haven.
William Collier, 1974, Sventoro, Guruwan and Makali, 'Agricultural Technology and Institutional Change in Java,' in *Food Research Institute Studies*, Vol. 13, No. 2, March, pp. 106 – 120.
William Collier, 1981, 'Agricultural Evolution in Java,' in Gary E. Hansen (ed.), *Agricultural and Rural Development in Indonesia*, Westview Press, Colorado.

9. Inayatullah (ed.), *Rural Organizations and Rural Development: Some Asian Experiences*, Asian and Pacific Development Administration Centre, Kuala Lumpur, Malaysia, 1978.

10. W. Collier, 1974, 1981, op. cit.

11. Ann Stoler, 'Rice Harvesting in Kali Loro: A Study of Class and Labour Relations in Rural Java'. Paper presented to the Annual Meeting of the American Anthropological Association, November 1976.

12. Collier, 1981, op. cit.

13. Ben White, 1981, 'Population Involution and Employment in Rural Java', in Hansen (ed.), op. cit.

14. Ibid.

15. J.K. Sundaram, 1977, 'Class Formation in Malaya: Capital, the State and Urban Development', Ph.D. Thesis, Harvard University.
Lim Teck Ghee, 1974, 'Peasant Agriculture in Colonial Malaya: Its Development in Perak, Selangor, Negeri Sembilan and Pahang, 1874 – 1941', Ph.D. Thesis, ANU.
W.E. Maxwell, 1884, 'Laws and Customs of the Malays with Reference to Land', in *Journal of the Straits Branch*, Royal Asiatic Society, Vol. 13.

16. Lorraine Corner, 1980, 'Mobility in the Context of Traditional Family and Social Relationships: Linkages, Reciprocity and Flow of Remittance. Malaysia: Padi Villages in Kedah Muda Region', 1980 Seminar Series, Development Studies Centre.
Ishak Shari, *et al.*, 1978, 'Rural – Urban Dimensions of Socio-Economic Relations in Northern Peninsular Malaysia: A Report from Two Village Studies', Paper presented to the UNCRD Colloquium on 'Rural – Urban Relations', Nagoya, Japan.
S. Husin Ali, 1975, *Malay Peasant Society and Leadership*, Oxford University Press, Kuala Lumpur.

17. S. Jegathesan, 1977, 'The Green Revolution and the Muda Irrigation Scheme: An Analysis of its Impact on the Size Structure and Distribution of Rice Farmer Incomes', Muda Agricultural Development Authority, Monograph No. 30.
Ishak Shari and Jomo K.S., 1980, 'Malaysia's Green Revolution in Rice Farming: Capital Accumulation and Technological Change in Peasant Society', Paper presented to the UNITAR Conference on Alternative Development Strategies and the Future of Asia, New Delhi.

18. A great deal of work has been done in the Philippines on employment changes as a result of the presence of IRRI at Los Banos. R.W. Herdt and C. Capule, 1983, 'Adoption, Spread and Production Impact of Modern Rice Varieties in Asia', IRRI, Los Banos, Philippines.
IRRI, 'Central Luzon Loop Survey Data for 1979', IRRI, Los Banos, Philippines.
J. Smith and F. Gascon, 1979, 'The Effect of the New Rice Technology on Family Labour Utilization In Laguna', IRRI, Research Paper Series No. 42, IRRI, Los Banos, Philippines.

19. R. Barker and R.W. Herdt, (forthcoming), *The Asian Rice Economy*, Johns Hopkins Press, U.S.A.

20. David C. Korten and Felipe B. Alfonso (eds), 1981, *Bureaucracy and the Poor*, Asian Institute of Management, McGraw Hill, Philippines.

M.J. Esman, 1972, *Administration and Development in Malaysia*, Cornell University Press.

21. NACIWID, 1978, 'Women in Development', Plan of Action.
22. RISDA, 1982, 'Kajian Sumbangan Kaum Wanita Kepada Pembangunan Masyarakat Pekebun Kecil Getah', Unit Penyelidikan Socio-Ekonomi.
23. Glen Williams and Satoto, 1980, 'Socio-Political Constraints on Primary health Care', in *Development Dialogue*, No. 1.
24. Iman Sudjahn and Anidal Hasjir, 1978, 'The Role of Formal and Informal Leaders' Wives at Serpang', in *Development of Women's Organizations in Rural Areas*, ESCAP, Bangkok.
25. Vinson H. Sutlive, 'The Many Faces of Kumang: Iban Women in Fiction and Fact', *Sarawak Museum Journal*, Vol. XXV, No. 46, 1977.

CHAPTER 3

Women, Migration and Income Generation

Introduction

In many parts of South-East Asia, the changes in the pattern of migration are striking. Traditionally, mostly the men would migrate for periods of short duration while their wives took care of the rural households. However, at present, more young women than men leave their rural base. Equally striking is the dominance of women migrants in specific forms of small-scale production and income-generating activities.

This chapter examines the subordination/emancipation theme by focusing on two important questions. First, why are more women migrating, and second, why are migrant women concentrated in very specific types of income-generating activities like small-scale marketing, trading and out-work.

Essentially, these questions deal with how conditions of production and accumulation are being organized and how the utilization of labour is regulated. In these processes, dominant ideologies regarding sex roles and women's position interact with economic factors to bring about the structuring of very specific social spaces for women. These factors include the restructuring of certain sectors of production and its effects on the economic activities and social position of women; the selective labour utilization in different branches of production; the ideological assumptions about the nature of women's work and the value placed on female labour power; the close inter-relationship between the domestic role of women within the household (i.e., their actual functioning within the household) and their position as specific kinds of income-generating workers.

Women and Migration

In South-East Asia, young women now form a major proportion of the rural—urban drift. The most recent published work in Thailand[1] showed that rural—urban migration is a highly selective process. The highest rates of movement occurred among single persons in the age group 25–29. Thirty-seven per cent of rural—urban migrants are under the age of 20 and 67 per cent are under the age of 25. There is a higher rate of movement for young women than for young males up to the age of 20. The higher mobility of Thai young women in this age group is also supported by census data.[2] These young rural women are more likely than their male counterparts to move to Bangkok where there is a greater demand for certain kinds of young female services, for example domestic service, masseuses, sexual services, 'entertainment' of various sorts in the night spots and restaurants of Bangkok. A study of rural women in Thailand found that substantial numbers of young rural girls were migrating from the poor regions of the North and North East to work as masseuses in Bangkok. In fact, 75 per cent of the girls who were interviewed in Bangkok came from these regions and 70 per cent of them came from farming families.[3]

A recent work done on the Philippines[4] reveals that women are numerically dominant in almosts all kinds of contemporary Philippine migration, and they constitute a large majority in the recent urbanward migration of teenage and young-adult cohorts. It was found that these migrants concentrated in the 'services' occupational category. In fact, seven out of ten females in this category are migrants, and more than half of these are young, single, recently migrated women. The bulk of the females in the services are 'domestics'.

Studies from Peninsular Malaysia[5] also show the emergence of a similar pattern of migration. Unlike the Philippines and Thailand, young women are not, as yet, the bulk of the rural – urban drift although they form a very significant part of it. A study on Malaysian migrants[6] shows that for the Malay *kampung* (village), poverty alone does not result in population movement. The land tenure system and the nature of rent payment under the feudal and semi-feudal systems have major influences on whether migration is chosen as a solution to rural poverty. Various studies have shown that while different social classes of peasants exist at the village level, a substantial proportion subsist below the poverty line, caught in various forms of debt bondage to the landlord and local moneylenders.[7] The possibility of migration for heads of households and male family members needed to work on the land is limited in such a situation especially when land is registered and transferable only through the male. At the same time, there are pressures for family members to seek opportunities to acquire cash income elsewhere due to the declining ability of the peasant economy to meet rural subsistence. These family members are often the young females – people who could be spared from the land without the loss of that land. Also currently, there is a demand in the urban centres for cheap female labour willing to work in labour-intensive industries of foreign subsidiaries.

The causes of migration, especially sex-selective migration, are complex. Usually they are related to limited resources and personal dissatisfaction. They also vary according to different social classes in rural communities. Generally, people belonging to small farming households tend to migrate in response to rural displacement, to the hope of increasing their contribution to the household income, to attain social mobility. Agricultural wage workers usually migrate in response to fluctuations in the labour market and are more prone to migrate as a result of unemployment. Wealthier farmers often can rely on their resources so their sons and daughters migrate primarily in search of educational and social mobility.

Why More Women Are Migrating

The issue of sex selectivity in migration does not allow any easy generalization. Efforts to explain the changing patterns of migration in South-East Asia must begin by placing women's work within the context of wider economic changes. In other words, the local agrarian structures within which the women are located must be linked to national and international structures in order to understand the nature of labour surplus created, and the development of the labour market which allows the absorption of only some of the available labour. Labour that is not absorbed survives through various forms of subsistence employment.

As seen in the previous chapter, the nature of employment in the rural areas of South-East Asian countries is undergoing fundamental changes due to the following factors: the introduction of new crops for the international market; the privatization of land with the corresponding loss of land by large sections of the rural population; a change in the nature of land tenure and land ownership and technical innovations and changes in methods of production. The intervention of international capital with its technically advanced systems of production often accelerates this transformation. Transformation may also occur through the intervention of the State with its political, bureaucratic and financial powers. Shifts in the land use and in structures of employment are accompanied by changes in skill requirements which do not necessarily absorb all those who were previously employed and new additions to the rural labour force because of population growth. Frequently the result is unemployment with corresponding pressures for the displaced population to use those existing skills they have by migrating in search of alternative employment.

These changes in the rural areas affect both women and men, though often in different ways, depending on the degree and nature of female participation in the agricultural system and on the nature of labour demand in the urban centres. The specific effect of the changes can only be determined by looking at concrete situations. While much of the evidence is still tentative, some effects of land pressure, decreasing rural resources and skill restructuring on the economic participation of women can be observed in South-East Asia. Women are squeezed out of agricultural production into casual labour and domestic labour. Women who are no longer able to make an important contribution to the agricultural economy often migrate out of rural areas, in search of alternatives elsewhere.

With economic changes, the division of labour by sex and age also changes. Fathers, brothers and eldest sons participate more in 'modern' agricultural tasks. At the same time, women's roles in traditional relationships and various groups get eroded as rural households become more dependent on bureaucracies which again are male-dominated. Traditional occupations of authority for rural women are also disappearing without the emergence of new ones. The traditional midwife, the traditional masseuses, healers and spirit mediums are being replaced by modern hospital assistants, nurses and doctors from the urban areas.

Another factor is that of land fertility. With intensive cultivation, land rapidly loses its fertility and gives small yields without the application of chemical fertilizers, which can be costly. Many families, in order to be competitive have also increased mechanization which has reduced the need for labour but increased the need for cash.

Pressures are set for children of these families to migrate in search of cash income. These pressures, together with the new employment opportunities for young women in urban factories, encourage families to send daughters out of rural areas.

Traditional means of earning cash income for women in rural areas are declining as they are taken over by larger commercial enterprises and monopolistic activities of urban merchants. Together with this are new services which must be paid for like electricity, irrigation water, and extra funds required at school even if education is free. In addition, new consumption patterns advocated by mass advertising have also increased the desire to acquire goods such as radios, watches, manufactured clothes, and others.

Increasingly, because land is being inherited by the males, women are being excluded from family property. The fact that women do not inherit directly reinforces the economic and social hardships of unmarried, widowed or divorced women. All these factors create pressures for young women to migrate especially in areas where the marginalization of women's labour in agricultural areas occurs side by side with the demand for specific (i.e., young) female labour in urban areas such as the growth of assembly lines, textile factories, the demand for domestic help, the growth in the traffic of young women in sex-related occupations.

Besides the factors mentioned, there is sufficient evidence to indicate that female migration is not only related to factors of production but equally important to social relations of gender. Many older women who migrate in South-East Asia are divorced, separated or have husbands who have taken minor wives (e.g. in Thailand).

Perhaps the best documented case of the relationship of the social relations of gender and female migration is the migration of Chinese women from mainland China to South-East Asia. The lives of Chinese women were influenced not just by economic factors but also by the dominant ideology of traditional Chinese society. This dominant ideology was strongly linked to the cosmological foundations which saw the universe as composed of two interacting elements – the female 'yin' and the male 'yang'. The yin is made up of all that is dark, weak and passive in contrast to the yang which is made up of all that is bright, strong and active. The yin/yang cosmology was incorporated into Confucian teachings which saw the role of woman as one of complete submission and compliance, particularly to her husband ('A husband, he is Heaven') and his family.[8] After marriage a woman came under the authority of her mother-in-law in all domestic matters and was often harshly treated by her. Many women of all classes feared marriage, but particularly the rural women who would have to work harder than other classes for her husband's family as there would be no servants to help them.[9]

In South China, especially Kwangtung and Fukien provinces where women have traditionally worked in the fields, worked as coolies and as other casual workers, protest against this marriage system was much louder than in Northern China as was their protest against foot-binding. This protest against the traditional marriage system did not attack the system as such nor was there any attempt to change it. Instead the women simply refused to marry. In the Sun Tak district of Kwangtung, they joined a movement called 'girls who do not go to the family'. Most of these girls worked in silk factories and were economically independent. So strong was the pressure for marriage that many of these women became 'women who put their own hair up', that is, they coiled their hair into buns like married women. During this ceremony they would invite their friends and relatives to a 'marriage feast' to announce that they were 'as if married' and hence could not be forced into real marriage. Many of these girls had to pay large compensation to their would-be husbands' families as a substantial number of them were promised in marriage when very young. Even with compensation the man's family frequently caused trouble for the girl, particularly if she remained in the same district to work. The rejection of marriage was a great loss of face for the man and his family. Hence from 1933 when female migration to Malaya and Singapore was encouraged, shiploads of Cantonese women, mostly from the Sun Tak and Dun Kwan districts, came to Malaya and Singapore. Between 1934 and 1938, 190,000 Chinese women had migrated. In Singapore many of these women worked as domestic servants, organizing themselves into associations and remained unmarried.[10]

Whatever the macro-pressures are, women will migrate only if they individually choose to do so. Some of the reasons given at the individual level by young women who migrate are to 'try their luck', 'tired of rural life', 'escaping from relatives', 'sick of the hard work', 'to make some money', 'to meet better men'. In short, women migrate to escape from their poor positions in the social and economic systems which limit their creative participation and as a strategy to increase their opportunities and resources. The extent to which they can actually do so is another issue.

The Women Left Behind

It is incomplete to examine women and migration without discussing at least briefly the effect of male migration on the women left behind in the villages. Even when women are married to men who inherit land, difficulties exist if the men are small-scale farmers. Many men inherit plots that are too small to support a family. In Thailand, for example, many rural families are displaced by dam construction, and irrigation projects. Also the average amount of land per family in Thailand has dropped from 16 to 14 rai between 1973 and 1975. At the same time, the number of agricultural families is increasing. Between 1960 and 1976, the number increased from 3.7 to 5.1 million.[11]

The productivity of agriculture has been increased by the intensive use of inputs such as water, fertilizers, pesticides, new seed varieties, multiple cropping, which are not only costly but also depend on a number of changes in social and economic structure, (e.g., the land tenure systems) before they can benefit poor farmers. Given the unlikelihood of these changes occurring and the real possibilities of widening income distribution, many men seek migration as a solution, leaving their wives in the villages.

What is the effect of a male's absence on the economic and social roles of women left behind? Do they gain new status or do they continue in their traditional roles? Information on these issues is limited.

In Thailand it has been found that marriage limits female mobility far more than it does males. Documentation of six villages of Roi-et Province showed that 39 per cent of married male heads of households aged between 30 and 39 had moved to urban centres during the three-year period covered by the research compared to 4 per cent of females in this age group who were married. In these villages, rice farming is highly seasonal with two annual peaks of labour inputs – July and August for planting and December for harvesting. In each year the highest rates of absence occur often after the harvest and before the planting season. However, it was found that this type of seasonal migration was restricted to the older married males rather than the younger group who tend to stay on in the towns.

Male migration from the rural areas may in fact change the power structure within the rural household in favour of the women who are left behind. These rural households are headed by women in the absence of a migrant male. These women are often in charge of their households and make most of the decisions about their land and crop. While the absence of men has undoubtedly given the rural women more authority within their households, these women have not gained status relative to other men in the village. Also, with long periods of male migration, family fragmentation often results especially in societies where males take 'minor wives'. When this happens, remittance to the rural household becomes irregular and there is a greater economic burden on the women left behind. In order to prevent this situation from occurring, some women visit their husbands regularly if they work in nearby towns, and may eventually migrate themselves.

Women Migrants and Work

The decision to migrate is only one part of the story. Another is the nature of the work of migrant women in urban areas. Their form of work is very much dependent on the wider economic situation which determines differential labour absorption in the urban areas, as well as dependent on the stage of the women's life cycle and their educational background.

Differential Labour Absorption and Women's Work

The economies of many South-East Asian countries are at a stage of development where the growth of stable wage employment is insufficient to absorb the high growth in population, so that certain groups (particularly women migrants) are incorporated at the margins of the urban economy. It has often been argued that in such a situation, hierarchical differences are utilized to organize the conditions of production and accumulation. In this section I look at some of these hierarchical differences and how they may contribute to the concentration of women in the low-income non-wage sector.

First, a 'labour aristocracy' has developed in many Third World countries, with high wages for small numbers of workers in the face of considerable excess labour supply. What results is a highly segmented labour market in which the labour force is separated into sub-markets with different employment conditions and wages. Access to high-wage jobs is not only dependent on being competent in certain skills but also related to the protection and bargaining power of organized labour. These frequently male-dominated trade unions often succeed in defining certain jobs as 'skilled' or as 'men's jobs' and therefore reduce the range of available jobs for women.

The issue of schooling takes on a new significance with the growth of a 'protected' labour market, particularly for employment in international manufacturing and clerical jobs in newly-created bureaucracies. In these labour markets, schooling and the credentials it provides are used as a selection mechanism and as a measure of labour's trainability and discipline. This has particular consequences. Access to schooling in low-income families often is sex-specific. It is frequently the male child who continues with his education while the female child drops out to substitute work for schooling or to reduce the financial cost of schooling within the household unit. The use of education as a screening mechanism, in this case, effectively excludes a substantial portion of women from stable employment.

Secondly, we need to consider the creation of an age-specific female workforce. In several Third World countries, the international fragmentation of the labour process has led to differential labour selection of women in different stages of their life cycle, that is to the creation of an age-specific labour force. There has been an overwhelming concentration of young women in world market factories, i.e., factories which export to the international market. A study published recently found that out of 103 Third World countries examined, 51 had World Market Factories (WMFs) where young women between the ages of 14 and 24 made up 70 per cent and more of the total employees.[12] In some countries, this percentage may be as high as 80 to 90 per cent of the factory workforce.[13]

The emergence of this particular type of world market factory represents a relocation of certain production processes from the developed countries to the Third World, particularly in the field of electronics and textiles. This type of relocation is based on product specialization which separates the labour-intensive processes from the research and design processes. Components or sub-components may be transported to various parts of the world where they undergo a range of labour-intensive processing. In short, what takes place is a kind of sub-contracting on the international level; skills and knowledge being retained in the developed countries while standardized activities are exported to Third World countries.

An analysis of differential labour absorption has to consider why, in some conditions and not in others, women are brought into employment in different branches of production. In this case, why the young women are introduced into production as cheap and productive labour.

For the above process of relocation to be highly profitable it is essential that production in terms of unit cost be as cheap as possible and that the nature of the workforce inspire confidence in the safety of the operation.[14] Female labour is almost always cheaper than the same category of male labour; for example, in Hong Kong, women's wages in the textile factories were about 30 per cent lower than those of a similar category of male workers; in South Korea, they are about 47 per cent lower.[15] As young women, they are classified in the labour market as 'secondary workers', and unlike male workers, are paid subsistence wages which do not cater for the reproduction of the family. The high concentration of young women in these industries is examined in greater detail in Chapter 6.

To summarize very briefly, the process of development has produced an 'uprooting' of rural groups and their redistribution to areas which provide some industrial and service sector employment. The groups that are selectively absorbed in stable wage employment are those with some educational qualifications and those who possess the characteristics demanded by 'modern sector employment'. These are usually male and young female workers. The group most discriminated against are older, often married women with few educational qualifications or formal documents. These women are hence forced to seek forms of non-wage income-generating activities. The next section looks at the details of this non-wage subsistence employment and seeks to explain why the economic participation of these women take their specific forms in these sectors.

Forms of Women's Income-Generating Activities

In many South-East Asian societies, the ability of women to participate in income-generating activities depends on their ability to manage multiple roles. In fact women's income-generating activities differ from those of men's in a variety of ways: first, they are concentrated in areas of the non-wage sector that are compatible with their reproductive role, particularly child-rearing, and often extensions of their domestic responsibilities within the household; secondly, they are with few exceptions concentrated in areas which require very little capital outlay and in areas with lesser growth potential.

Women in Trading and Marketing

In income-generating activities in the urban centres of South-East Asia, particularly in the two most important forms − selling of cooked food and petty trading − the following trends in the sexual division of labour have been widely noted.

Studies that have been done on the sexual divisions of labour in a number of income-generating activities in urban centres of South-East Asia found that the kinds of income-generating, non-wage labour in which low-income women are concentrated are those which involve skills developed within the household. The tasks entailed in unremunerated domestic labour (i.e., work carried out mainly by women in the home) are transferred to the wider economy where production is for exchange. Men, on the other hand, do work which involves 'new' skills (new to traditional South-East Asian village society) learned in the formal or non-formal educational systems or on the fringes of the modern industrial economy, for example, machine repairing. Men's economic activity in the informal sector also requires a higher capital investment than women's, such as the owning of small shops or owning a taxi or van.

In South-East Asia one of the most common forms of income-generating activity for women is trading in cooked food. This work can be carried out by women in their own homes and be part of family consumption. Many women cook within their own premises. Cooking is a frequent choice for woman particularly if she is the head of her household. It requires very little initial capital outlay; it makes use of traditional skills; it allows a woman to combine her livelihood with her child-raising function, and it is more lucrative than many of the jobs open to women with little formal education.

Comparisons of the marketing activities of women in relation to those of men, show a tendency for women to concentrate in areas which provide lower returns: thus in a Singapore market it was found that women were concentrated in the vegetable section, while the men were concentrated in the meat and fish section which brought higher rates of return.[16] Even in the black market of Rangoon, Burma, where smuggled goods are traded, there is a sexual division of labour. My brief visit to Bogyoke Aung San Market, where most of this trading is done, showed that women are concentrated in the 'safer areas' e.g. textiles, garments, cosmetics, while the men deal in the more dangerous and hence high income areas like gems, medicinal drugs, antiques. The women also generate income by standing in queues for others to buy goods from government stores. In the actual smuggling of goods from the Thai boarder, the dealers are men while women are used as carriers of the goods.

In many parts of South-East Asia women were concentrated in small-scale trading while men were involved with large-scale trading. The main reason for this is not only the lack of access to markets, trading contacts and transportation, but also the fact that large-scale trading required a level of flexibility and mobility that women did not have unless they were freed from their domestic chores.

In a village study done in Jogdjakarta, Java, one of the poorest regions in the world, it was found that over 60 per cent of the women in the survey were engaged in trading, preparation of food for sale and crafts as their primary occupation as opposed to about 10 per cent of the men interviewed. Most of the men (65 per cent), on the other hand, were employed as farmers and salaried officials as compared to 17 per cent of the women.[17] The activities of these women traders in fact allowed the men to sell their labour at a sub-subsistence family wage in a situation of labour surplus.

In most South-East Asian cities, the trading and marketing activities of women take place at street corners, lucrative roadsides, market places or *pasar malam* (night markets). These activities can be extremely competitive. New migrants or women new to trading have great difficulty in being accepted into a lucrative area. New traders are often forced to become mobile sellers, moving from place to place or selling in 'illegal sites' where they risk arrest and having their goods confiscated by the police who occasionally check these areas for unlicensed hawkers.

While a rigid sexual division of labour does not exist in small-scale marketing and trading, it is the woman who usually helps out in the husband's small retail shop as an unpaid family worker, together with her children. When women are encouraged in the business of trading in their own right, they are often involved in activities that do not require large capital outlay, require less helpers and hence are less profitable.

Women in Outwork

Outwork involves putting out all or part of the production process from a central point to several small units. This process is part of the strategy to cut labour costs, to overcome problems of capital investment and to survive in a competitive market. By putting out its work, the central enterprise takes advantage not only of low wages, insecurity of employment, and lack of social benefits but also of long working hours.

Outworkers in South-East Asia are predominantly women and children. Because they are usually external to the enterprise, they are overlooked by governments, trade unions and data collectors. These women often perform the finishing and assembling processes in their own homes for particular industries, for example, footwear, clothing, food and now even electronics. The presence of these outworkers enables the factory to employ a small core staff. Although these homeworkers are often the main income earners of their households for all purposes they are regarded as 'housewives' who 'do not work'. Producers pay these women very low wages because the ideological assumption is that as women they must be secondary earners and dependent on their husbands.

Thailand has a long tradition of skilled garment workers in the North involved in embroidery. This embroidery is done in the premises of the women's homes. The women are also likely to be assisted by other family members with daughters and mothers as chief helpers. The work put in by relatives is unpaid. Payment is made on a piece-rate basis and is very low, not at all in accordance with the level of skill involved. For example, for the embroidery of one dress, a woman gets 5 bahts. Payment coincides with the collection of the finished goods and delivery and collection are carried out by the contractor who supplies the urban markets with cheap clothing. Children's embroidered dresses are sold for 30 – 35 bahts a piece.

In Bangkok itself, the organization of outwork takes a different form. Garment workers work in the premises of shophouses under the supervision of male employers who own the garment shops. In order to secure a minimum income, many of the young women employed in these shops work at a punishing pace with their sewing machines.

An important question at this stage is why some men in the informal sector manage to be self-employed and even small-scale employers while women with their skills seldom attain the status of independent producers? This question can only be fully answered if we examine dominant ideologies regarding sex roles and women's position.

Traditionally, in South-East Asia, especially in areas where Chinese influence has been strong, a woman is ideologically defined as an 'inside person' and hence has had very little physical mobility and outside contacts compared to the man. Women of peasant households tend to move freely but they are classified as 'rough women'. Also, although peasant women are active in production, their productive roles are confined to the households and domestic cottage industry.

This ideology about sex roles and women's position continues to the present in the sense that for many women the household is still the most important sphere. And the aspiration to be independent is related to independence within the household. Hence, many women outworkers working within the confines of the home feel that they have relatively more freedom than those working in office premises. This is probably due to their multiple roles as wife, mother and worker. A woman's understanding of freedom is conditioned by her feeling of responsibility for the home as much as an income earner. A man is also conditioned to care for his family but his care is ideologically expected to be shown by providing for the family through outside work. In other words, a man is not ideologically tied to the household and is expected to define his manhood outside the sphere of the household.

Given this situation, women, even those with skills, are excluded from knowledge of large-scale marketing and contacts. They also have less ability to command the labour of the household in the same way as men. Because of women's secondary status, it is very unlikely that the entire household will organize itself around the work of a woman. She may be able to draw support from her daughters and female relatives, but seldom from male members for long periods. For all these reasons, women's outwork remains at a particular status – the status of informality that blends with domesticity.

Women in Domestic Service

Another form of work that is a complete extension of tasks performed by women within the household is domestic service. Although in countries like India with a large labour surplus, some males are employed as domestic servants, such employment is predominantly a female occupation. This form of employment is one where women are already skilled as a result of task allocation by the sexual division of labour within the household. The tasks are practically the same ones performed as unpaid work within the family – cleaning, washing, ironing and taking care of children. Although domestic service is a relatively stable wage employment and cannot be strictly described as informal sector employment, it has some features similar to most informal sector jobs, for instance it is work done without a written contract and therefore the employee may be subjected to instant dismissal; it is work that is seldom protected by any government regulations. Domestic service is the frequent job choice for female migrants and poor urban women, being readily available because of the growth of a large middle class. Despite many insecure features of domestic service, the experience of Singapore appears to show that the conditions of women in this type of employment are not static but are closely linked to the growth of the economy and the availability of labour.

Before industrialization, domestic servants were a part of the majority of middle class and all upper class households. The conditions of work differed according to whether the person employed was considered as a 'skilled' or 'unskilled' servant. When male persons (usually the Hainanese) were employed by colonial families or by local upper class families as cooks, they were defined as relatively skilled and freed from the constant supervision that young female servants were subjected to. These male cooks were employed together with their families. Their jobs were task-specific – they did the cooking and their wives the cleaning. Unlike married men, married women are almost never employed as live-in servants especially if they have children. They are usually employed on a part-time basis. The live-in female servants may be differentiated into the fairly elderly, single, widowed or separated 'Cantonese Asam' – the skilled female servants; and the rest, the bulk of whom are the young single girls – the unskilled servants. The Cantonese Asam has the protection of her guild and the unwritten understanding with the employing household is that this servant cannot be subject to instant dismissal, she must have control over her labour activities and her labour cannot be called upon after a certain hour of the night. These conditions of employment have a long history linked to the protection these women have obtained through collective organization.

Many of the Cantonese Asams were people who were actively involved in the anti-marriage movement referred to earlier. In Singapore, they organized themselves into associations along the Cantonese dialects line, remained unmarried, often adopting young girls to look after them in their old age. All the Cantonese Asams live together in the premises of the association. If one of their members experiences ill treatment from her employer, no other member would offer services to that employer. The services of the Cantonese Asam have traditionally been highly valued in Singapore society. Not only are these women regarded as loyal and reliable, but they are highly skilful in cooking. Also there are only a limited number of such people as they are a 'dying group' disappearing because of the rapid changes in Singapore society.

The conditions of service rendered to the Cantonese Asams are completely lacking when the young single girls are employed. For a long time it was common knowledge that many of these young girls were badly treated by their mistresses, subjected to beatings and accusations of theft. It was only by the early 1970s that the pattern of employment for young women began to change. There was a massive mobilization of young women on a scale never before experienced by the country, because of the spread of foreign labour-intensive subsidiaries – electronics and textiles – looking urgently for a workforce to work for low wages in semi-skilled and unskilled jobs. Under the label of 'female emancipation', local unpaid labour from household chores, from orphanages and social welfare homes (the main suppliers of young domestic servants) and domestic service were converted into industrial wage labour. Because of the bargaining power obtained from the existence of alternative sources of employment, wages of domestic servants in Singapore have increased very substantially, and certain conditions of employment for young servants have improved, for example, shorter working hours and weekend leave. Although these new conditions are not translated into laws of employment and made legally binding, they are transmitted as commonly understood informal rules. This informality makes for some insecurity as these benefits may disappear as quickly as they have appeared. Currently, due to the shortage of local women willing to work in domestic service, this sector is filled by teachers and even college graduates from countries like Sri Lanka, the Philippines, Indonesia and Thailand.

In Malaysia, young single women may work for a while as live-in domestic help but later shift over to outwork or a factory job. Women with dependants are employed by several households in the mornings as part-time maids, involved with washing and ironing of clothes as well as general cleaning of the houses. During this time the children would be left behind with a neighbour in the slums, squatter area or estate at a small cost. This arrangement prevents women in need of income from being 'trapped' in their homes because of young children.

The situation in Bangkok is more complex. There are different kinds of domestic help. The most highly paid are those that work for foreigners. Income can be as high as 3,500 bahts a month. The lowest least paid are new rural migrants working in local homes. Some of them are paid as low as 300 bahts a month, especially if the household employs more than one maid. Often maids in rich local households work in groups with clearly defined tasks and hierarchy. The 'Number One Maid' would usually be in charge of cooking and supervision of other maids who would be involved with general cleaning.

Women's Networks as a Survival Strategy

I am concerned here with how life goes on for households in urban poverty. The reproduction of life is precarious in these households. Besides turning to income-generating activities, women especially in crisis situations turn to complex networks of kin and neighbours as a survival strategy. It may be that some women in extremely impoverished conditions are still able to raise healthy children while others are not mainly because the former group has access to various survival networks while the second group does not.

In South-East Asia, there seem to be three patterns at work:

1. Although the family system has frequently been a system of sexual inequality and many women have sought to escape from oppressive family relationships, it is often the family and kinship systems which are recreated even by women, hopefully without the negative features of the system, in their attempts to deal with the problems of poverty and survival.

2. Besides the family and kinship system, new social groups are created for mutual support. These social groups take various forms. They may be neighbourhood groupings of supportive households; they may be people joined together by a shared, newly-created ideology; they may be people who are linked together by a common religion.

3. The creation of vertical linkages with social groups that are financially more stable. The most common form is the patron–client relationship.

A number of studies have shown how relationships are activated and used for acts of exchange. The urban poor, as a survival strategy, organize their relationships as a social capital that also substitutes for the credentials and organized careers of the formal economy.

In a situation of poverty, when life is extremely insecure, it is important to have automatic support in times of crisis. Family and kinship systems have commonly been used as unambiguous pointers as to who had the rights to assistance in times of need. These systems have not been without conflict, domination and violence, but they at least provided their members with some social insurance.

When the overseas Chinese were thrown together in a strange setting in Singapore and Malaysia, they created territorial surname and dialect associations as new forms of social groups. These new groups were run on kinship principles, furnishing the migrants with assistance when in need. The surname association in particular brought together large numbers of kinsmen in a new setting for secular and religious co-operation. Besides these groups which were common to both men and women, special sex-specific groups existed. Among the men, the secret societies (before they became criminal groups with the aim of robbery and extortion) furnished them with assistance, organized their funerals, defended their rights and acted as a faithful brotherhood. For the women, equally strong associations of sisterhoods grew up. These sisterhoods were strongest among the Hakka and Cantonese women, working as casual labourers on building sites, as domestic servants, and as small-scale traders (hawkers) selling cooked and uncooked food. These sisterhoods consciously retained the old ideas of family and kinship life. They were often substitute families where extensive and intricate family relationships existed among members of the same sex.[18]

Besides these sisterhoods, many unmarried or widowed women sought help and sanctuary in religious institutions particularly in vegetarian houses or *chai tang*.[19]

The manipulation of social networks for survival has also been documented in parts of Indonesia. Various studies of women's income-generating activities in Indonesia indicate that the ability of women to participate in income-generating activities depends on their ability to manage multiple roles. Her ability to manage multiple roles, that is, to manage with child-raising and household maintenance depends on the availability of other women and sometimes her husband to help with household chores.

As an example the structure provided by the extended family has facilitated women's involvement in trade. The existence of several female persons within the household allows the practice of a division of labour in domestic duties, so that all can have some time to carry out some trading, mat-making, etc. Women's trading capacity is very much affected by the extent they are free from domestic work. The pattern of sharing household chores and child-rearing responsibilities gives all women some time to trade.

Studies of slum communities in Thailand also show the great reliance placed on kinship and neighbourhood mutual-aid networks for low-cost housing, certain market circuits of goods, services and labour. Because of the lack of a family wage and the highly restricted access to credit facilities, low-income households survive by creating as much security as possible within the limits of the larger structures. One common way is the creation of vertical linkages, for example, the creation of patron – client relationships. This relationship has all the obligations, tensions and conflicts associated with an unequal relationship. However, it ensures at least simple accumulation. Unlike the better-off classes, who have more choices, the poor are often forced to endure tensions and conflicts in relationships for the sake of basic survival.

Conclusion

Because of the changing structure of rural employment and its effect on women's position, more women are now migrating in South-East Asia. Most of these women are young, but there are also single women with children, women married to men in the lowest income brackets and older unmarried, divorced and widowed women, who are dependent upon their own persons. The concentration of migrant women in certain types of income-generating activity is largely the result of larger structural and ideological forces in restricting the demand for particular kinds of women workers in the labour market, for example, women without the appropriate educational titles or women with young children. For many of these women working is a matter of survival. They therefore enter into subsistence production, depending on whatever skills they already have. These skills are closely related to the domestic sphere and to the traditional sexual division of labour within the household. Consequently, the nature of work of these women takes very specific forms – forms that allow the combination of work and child care, forms that are extensions of women's domestic responsibilities within the household, forms that require little capital outlay, forms that do not threaten the boundaries constructed by traditional ideology governing sex roles.

While forms of work are directed by structural and ideological systems, women are seldom passive agents of these forces. Their economic behaviour in response to these forces take different forms. There remain differences in interpretation and organization of social experience, and the resistance to larger processes which may range from highly individualist, competitive solutions (e.g., individual small-scale traders and food-sellers competing in the market place) to solutions that are managed and controlled in a collective manner (as particularly shown in the case of the Cantonese Asams or skilled domestic servants). Whatever the solution, however, there appears to be very great reliance on privately created (as opposed to nationally created) systems that can be used as unambiguous pointers to rights of assistance in time of crisis. These systems range from family and kinship systems and newly created mutual aid networks of different sorts, to patron–client relationships. These networks do not bring about any long-term fundamental changes in regard to problems of emancipation and even of poverty, but in the short term they at least provide some guarantee of survival, particularly during periods of great hardship.

Notes and References

1. Theodore D. Fuller, *et al.*, 1983, *Migration and Development in Modern Thailand*, Social Science Association of Thailand, Bangkok.
2. Quoted in Fuller, *et al.*, 1983.
3. Phongpaichit, P., 1980, 'Rural Women of Thailand: From Peasant Girls to Bangkok Masseuses', *ILO Working Paper*, WEP 10/WP 14, Geneva.
4. Evoita and Smith, 1979, 'The Migration of Women in the Philippines', Unpublished paper presented to the Working Group on 'Women in Cities', East-West Centre, Hawaii.
5. Heyzer, Noeleen, 1979, 'From Rural Subsistence to an Industrial Peripheral Workforce: An Examination of Female Malaysian Migrants and Capital Accumulation in Singapore', in Lourdes Beneria (ed.), *Women and Employment*, ILO, Geneva.
   Jamilah, M.A., 1980, 'Female Labour Migration to Urban-based Factories in Malaysia and Malay Women's Participation in the Labour Force', Unpublished paper presented at the Workshop on 'Analysis of Female Migration', East-West Centre, Hawaii.
6. Heyzer, 1979, op. cit.
7. S. Husin Ali, 1975, *Malay Peasant Society and Leadership*, Oxford University Press, Kuala Lumpur.
   Swift, M.C., 1965, *Malay Peasant Society in Jelebu*, Athlone Press, London.
   Dahlan, 'Micro-Analysis of Village Communities in Peninsular Malaysia: A Study of Under-development', in H.M. Dahlan (ed.), *The Nascent Malaysian Society*, Kuala Lumpur, 1976.
8. Croll, E., 1978, *Feminism and Socialism in China*, Routledge and Kegan Paul, London.
9. Topley, Marjorie, 1954, 'Chinese Women's Vegetarian Houses in Singapore', *Journal of the Malayan Branch, Royal Asiatic Society*, Vol. 27, Part 1, pp. 51–67.
10. Topley, 1954, op. cit.
11. FAO, 1979, 'Migration and Rural Development', FAO Economic and Social Development Paper No. 8, Rome.

12. Frobel, F., J. Heinrichs and O. Kreye, 1977, Die Neue Internationale Arbeitsteiung (The International Division of Labour), Reinbek bei Hamburg.

13. Lim, L., 1978, 'Women Workers and MNCs in Developing Countries: The Case of the Electronics Industry in Malaysia and Singapore', Occasional Paper No. 9, University of Michigan.
    Heyzer, Noeleen, 1983, 'The Relocation of International Production and Low-pay Female Employment: The Case of Singapore', in Young, K., *Serving Two Masters*, Routledge and Kegan Paul, London.

14. Elson, D. and Pearson, 1980, 'The Internationalisation of Capital and Its Implications for Women in the Third World', IDS Discussion Paper.

15. Yoon, S.Y., 1979, 'The Halfway House – MNCs. Industries, and the Asian Factory Girls', mimeo, UNAPDI, Bangkok.

16. Lim, Charlotte, 1980, 'The Position of Women in Market-place Trade in a Modern City State', mimeo, Sociology Department, University of Singapore.

17. White, B., 1976b, 'Population, Involution and Employment in Rural Java', in Gary E. Hansen, (ed.), *Agricultural Development in Indonesia*, Cornell University Press.

18. Freedman, M., 1957, *'Chinese Family and Marriage in Singapore'*, Athlone Press London.
    Freedman, M., 1958, *Lineage Organisation in Southeastern China*, Athlone Press, London.

19. Topley, 1954, op. cit.

CHAPTER 4

The Trade in Female Sexuality

Introduction

Another work situation commonly classified as part of the 'informal sector' is one that relies on the trade in female sexuality. The phenomenal growth of young women in this employment in many South-East Asian countries in recent years is often linked to the highly organized promotion of tourism in these countries. When evaluated from the viewpoint of economic growth, tourism means big business. In 1978, 270 million international tourists in the world were estimated to have spent more than US\$ 75 billion.[1] Many countries in South-East Asia are now looking at tourism as an important factor in national economic prosperity. Tourism has become a very major industry and quick source of foreign exchange in several South-East Asian countries and may overtake many other commodities to become one of the largest single items of international trade.

In addition to turning to tourism as an important source of foreign currency surplus, many governments are also using tourism as a development strategy in the generation of employment and as a stimulus for the growth of the domestic economy. The tourist industry is seen by governments as a potentially effective means to diversify the economy, to contribute towards regional development, to provide employment both directly and indirectly, to stimulate the development of other supplying industries and to stimulate the revival and expansion of traditional handicrafts and cultural forms.[2] However, the nature of employment generated locally is completely dependent on the nature of demands for goods and services by the foreign traveller. Tourism is essentially a service industry; the pursuit of leisure, entertainment, cultural enrichment, traditional handicrafts – and it is in these areas that employment is generated and foreign exchange earned.

A variety of jobs is created for both men and women in the hotel chains, in tourist complexes, in the airline systems, in traditional and modern entertainment and in the souvenir industry. The jobs for young women are usually concentrated in public relations, in the promotional aspects of tourism, as cashiers and waitresses, in traditional entertainment, in new entertainment and servicing including sexual servicing demanded by visitors and by business tourists, the bulk of whom are men. The major varieties of female images used in the promotion of tourism range from the traditional woman, the graceful, smiling, docile female, to the image of the sexual woman, portrayed in the role of the temptress. Recently, much controversy has arisen surrounding the question of sex tourism.

The well advertised entertainment offered by bar girls, a-go-go dancers, turkish bath attendants and masseuses is often a thin disguise of the actual prostitution market, further thinned down by advertisements featured in sex-tour brochures of which the following caption is a common example:

> Thailand is a world full of extremes, and the possibilities are limitless. Anything goes in this exotic country – especially when it comes to girls. Yet visitors to Thailand cannot always find the exciting places where they can indulge in unknown pleasures. It is frustrating to have to ask the hotel receptionist in broken English where you can pick up pretty girls. Rosie Reisen has come up with the answer. For the first time in history you can book a trip to Thailand with erotic pleasures included in the price. . . .[3]

Sex tourism is only an instance among many other enterprising systems that draw income from the trade in female sexuality. The sex-tour clients are individuals, small groups of friends or even large groups of men sent by their employers to sex holiday resorts as a form of company bonus.[4] They may choose the woman from picture books before departure, select them in person or pick them out by pointing at pinned numbers. The soft bland image of an oriental culturally exotic but uninhibited girl is frequently used to draw the tourist's attention:

> For all her exuberance, frivolity and easy laughter, even the girl working within Thailand's entertainment industry remains traditionally Thai. . . . A young girl with long black hair in a sequined bikini and high heels lights incense and walks across the room to place it on a Buddhist shrine. But, as she walks, she cannot resist swaying a bit to the incessant sound of the latest taped music.[5]

The planned effect of such advertisements, and the comforts of well organized tourism combines with the appealing attraction of the anonymous atmosphere of a foreign country to provide male tourists with the novelty of a different experience as well as with a safe release from the constraints of familiar social codes and customs.

But while tourism increases the dividends of the prostitution market, it is by no means totally responsible for its flourishing and maintenance. For it is known that prostitution caters to local as well as foreign consumption and its practice is primarily supported and tolerated by indigenous ideological, socio-economic and political systems. Female sexuality and its expression at different functional levels thus falls under direct control, exerted by interacting variables, within such systems.

Any effort at assessing in accurate numbers the extent of the sex trade in the South-East Asian region, or even less ambitiously in particular countries, results at best in mere approximate figures. The many deficiencies inherent in statistical data on women in this sector are pronounced. Relevant data is often very misleading and suffers largely from thin assumptions; and existent fragmented information rests mainly on confined area surveys undertaken by government groups such as police, medical and social welfare teams and private researchers.

TABLE 4.1   Establishments Linked With the Practice of Prostitution in Bangkok

119	massage parlours
119	barber-shop-cum-massage and tea-houses
97	night clubs
248	disguised whore houses
394	discos-cum-restaurants
977	Total

SOURCE: Thepanom Muangman *et al.*, Report of a study on education, attitude and work of 1,000 massage girls in Bangkok, with special reference to family planning, pregnancy, abortion, venereal disease and drug addiction. (Unpublished paper in Thai, Bangkok, 1980.)

Although the illegality of prostitution in most countries of the region and the fluidity of the scarce statistical data on its incidence prevents any truely accurate estimate of the number of women who engage in the practice, several estimates have been made. Estimates of the number of masseuses and prostitutes in Bangkok range from 100,000 to 200,000.[6] A Police Department estimate of the total number of masseuses and prostitutes in the whole of Thailand in 1965 is 400,000.[7] Another calculation concludes that 15,000 girls cater to demands by tourists in Bangkok.[8] The number of establishments linked with the practice of prostitution in Bangkok has been estimated at 977 (see Table 4.1).[9] In Manila, a survey carried out by the Bureau of Women and Minors in 1978 recorded 1,735 women working in the hospitality industry, 65 per cent of which were under 25 years of age (see Tables 4.2 and 4.3). Another report in the same country quotes 7,003 as the number of registered hospitality girls.[10] In Sri Lanka, according to official statistics from the Ministry of Plan Implementation, 481 female prostitutes were arrested and 465 were prosecuted in 1975 (see Table 4.4).[11] Apart from the data limitations already stated, caution must also be taken regarding the operational definitions behind these figures. Although the chances of overlapping are high, the term 'hospitality girl' or 'masseuse' are not always synonymous with prostitute.

A large number of the studies of prostitution focus primarily on the economics of the trade with some reference to the involvement of the tourist industry and of indigenous socio-cultural aspects, but touching less on psychological processes. With the aim of altering such tendencies, the following sections will not only look at prostitution as a practice but also at the prostitute as a person, her background, motives, aspirations, the risks she has to face, and her situation as it is affected by the system in which she operates.

The Prostitution Business

To understand the phenomenon of prostitution it is not sufficient to examine only the economic situation in which women find themselves but also the way prostitution becomes a business and who profits from it, how the profits are shared out, as well as the coercive structures which entangles women in the trade in female sexuality.

TABLE 4.2 Women Workers in the Hospitality Industry, by Civil Status, Manila

| Occupation | Total | | Civil Status | | | | | | | | | | |
| | | | Single | | Married | | Widowed | | Separated | | Unwed | | Not Stated | |
	Number	Per cent	Number	Per cent	Number	Per cent	Number	Per cent	Number	Per cent	Number	Per cent	Number	Per cent
Total	1,735	100.0	1,082	62.4	288	16.6	36	2.1	129	7.4	37	2.1	163	9.4
Masseuse	579	100.0	350	60.4	166	20.0	16	2.8	12	2.1	3	0.5	82	14.2
Hostess	548	100.0	320	58.4	99	18.1	13	2.4	57	10.4	9	1.6	50	9.1
Waitress	332	100.0	237	71.4	30	9.1	5	1.5	28	8.4	16	4.8	16	4.8
Taxi Dancer	164	100.0	112	68.3	17	10.4			28	17.1	5	3.0	2	1.2
Floor Manager	33	100.0	11	33.3	14	42.4	2	6.1	1	3.0			5	15.2
Countergirl	18	100.0	14	77.8	3	16.7					1	5.6		
A-go-go Dancer	15	100.0	13	86.6	1	6.7							1	6.7
Cashier	20	100.0	12	60.0	4	20.0			2	10.0	2	10.0		
Operator	3	100.0							1	33.3	1	33.3	1	33.3
Helper	3	100.0			2	66.7							1	33.3
Not Stated	20	100.0	13	65.0	2	10.0							5	25.0

NOTE: The Bureau of Women and Minors, Ministry of Labour and Employment, use the term 'hospitality girls' to include women employed as hostesses masseuses waitresses and dancers employed in nightclubs, cabaret, bars and similiar establishments.

SOURCE: Survey of women workers in the hospitality industry carried out by the Bureau of Women and Minors, Manila, 29 January – 31 March 1978.

TABLE 4.3 Young Women Workers in the Hospitality Industry, Manila, 1978

Occupation	Total Number	Per cent	Under 30 years (per cent)	Under 25 years (per cent)
Total	1,735	100.0	90.6	65.5
Masseuse	579	100.0	88.9	54.9
Hostess	548	100.0	91.1	64.3
Waitress	332	100.0	95.2	81.3
Dancers	179	100.0	93.9	82.7
Floor Manager	33	100.0	63.7	18.2
Cashier	20	100.0	90.0	65.0
Countergirls	18	100.0	100.0	83.7
Others	26	100.0	80.0	70.0

Prostitution: A Definition

By definition, the word prostitution carries a negative connotation exemplified by its frequent application as synonym of 'wrong' or 'unworthy use', a view particularly prominent in religious traditions that brand prostitutes as being in a sinful state devoid of religious and social grace. The value placed on the suppression of the young female's sex drive has been fundamental in stabilizing cultures around settled family life, and the emergence of prostitution under such a system, may be viewed as a one-sided outlet for the expression and reduction of male sex drive.

In one definition,[12] prostitution is seen as the engagement in sexual relations for non-amative considerations, which not only includes commercialized intercourse but also the bartering of sexual favours as well as sexual relations as mistresses whose primary motivation aims at pursuance of socio-economic benefits. Additional con-

TABLE 4.4 Reasons for Arrest, Sri Lanka, 1975

	Number Arrested			Number Prosecuted		
	Male	Female	Total	Male	Female	Total
1. Prostitutes	110	481	591	100	465	565
2. Brothels	121	181	302	120	178	298
3. Soliciting	22	301	323	22	239	261
4. Homosexuals	2	–	2	2	–	2
5. Narcotics (Ganja and Opium)	4,173	407	4,580	4,121	377	4,498
6. Sex Perversion						
(a) Exposure of person	26	3	29	26	3	29
(b) Peeping tom	2	–	2	2	–	2
(c) Molesting	99	–	99	99	–	99
7. Sale of Salacious cards Photographs and Pamphlets.	2	–	2	2	–	2

SOURCE: Statistics on Women and Development, Women's Bureau of Sri Lanka, Ministry of Plan Implementation, 15 May 1981.

siderations in attempts to define prostitution have include examination of the degree of promiscuity, indiscrimination and the exercise of a prerogative of refusal, voluntary as opposed to coercive action, economic as opposed to psychological needs, and the transiency and anonymity of the sexual encounter. While attempting to prevent value judgements or worse yet to take a professional moralizing stand, prostitution is here defined as a transaction by which a woman[13] engages in sexual interaction, with a transient partner for monetary gains. In this context, cash is the primary motivation and focal point in the interaction and power struggle between the prostitute, the client and all those other persons involved at intermediary levels of transaction, and the transiency and relative anomynity of the encounter accentuates the business nature of prostitution.

Background and Characteristics of Women in Prostitution

The social conditions under which women turn to prostitution is an important area for investigation. In S.E. Asian countries with exposure to huge military bases coupled with the unequal distribution of wealth and employment opportunities, various forms of the trade in female sexuality tend to flourish especially when there are acute pressures on women to earn an income.

While each girl has a unique set of motives and formative experiences that contribute to her agreeability for recruitment or her voluntary enlistment in prostitution, her entry may be viewed from three categories of causative factors. The first category, most basic to personality, is composed of internal predisposing factors such as loss of rigidity in the moral standards resulting in a self-concept that allows the choosing of prostitution as a career. The second one is composed of attracting factors involved in perceived comparative advantages of prostitution in terms of income, excitement of the life, approval or tolerance of prostitution in the immediate social milieu, and the expectation of sexual gratification. The last category is composed of precipitating factors which may include limitation of alternative courses of action, lack of opportunity for marriage, unemployment, lack of education, persuasion or coercion by a pimp or other prostitutes, and severe economic pressure. Predisposing and attracting factors, however, are less relevant in the case of very young women whose entry into prostitution is involuntary, a point that will be examined later in this chapter.

It has sometimes been argued that the economic rewards of prostitution tend to be greater than those of most other occupations open to unskilled and uneducated girls in South-East Asian countries. While no authoritative confirmation is possible, examples of economic enticement are multiple (see Table 4.5). A recent study of migrant Thai masseuses, stresses that these girls were not fleeing from a rural society that oppressed women but rather they were engaging in an entrepreneurial move to improve their economic situation.[14] The earnings enable the girls to look after themselves and, in some cases, to send cash or gifts to their relatives in the villages. In this way the loss of face for engaging in prostitution may be compensated or rationalized, and after some years in the trade, under the pressure of decreased demand due to aging, the women may go back to the village or integrate in conventional city life and become accepted by family and community. Some may even become Buddhist nuns to 'cleanse their mind'.[15]

TABLE 4.5   Income of a Sample of Masseuses

Masseuses' monthly income (Baht)	Number	Percentage
1,000 – 2,000	2	4
2,000 – 3,000	6	12
3,000 – 4,000	10	20
4,000 – 5,000	3	6
5,000 – 6,000	15	30
6,000 – 7,000	4	8
7,000 – 10,000	8	16
10,000 – 15,000	2	4
	50	100

NOTE: Information based on a sample of 50 masseuses.

SOURCE: Pasuk Phongpaichit, 'Rural Women of Thailand: From Peasant Girls to Bangkok Masseuses'. International Labour Office. World Employment Programme Research, 1980.

A measure of the psychological situation of women in prostitution is their perception of the attitudes and motives of their clients as well as their own attitudes and evaluation of the encounters. Such attitudes present wide variability, being more positive among the prettier, glamorous, and more successful girls who instead of succumbing to exploitation by pimps, agents and clients may be in a position to exploit their sexuality for profit. But the majority, those in the middle and lower ranks, and those operating in unprotective systems, tend to resign themselves to service customers on whom they look with disdain if not repressed hostility. Results of interviews in Bangkok by Phongpaichit on opinions of a small sample of masseuses about their clients showed that the majority (19 out of 30) thought that their customers were 'selfish', 'deceitful', people who 'cannot be trusted', 'boring', 'arrogant' or 'irresponsible'.

Defensive attitudes develop partly as a result of hostility against prostitution in the immediate social mileau. Feelings of shame in the eyes of others or of internalized guilt are often appeased by a variety of defence mechanisms. The women may resort to rationalization, projection, sublimation, reaction formation or other defences. The situation can be worsened by unwanted pregnancy and by the high risk of acquiring venereal disease, a condition that endangers not only their health and well-being but also that of their clients, and of their offspring in the event of future pregnancies. In Manila, 'hospitality girls' are given health certificates (see table 4.6) to show that they are free of diseases.

Different Forms of Prostitution

From the point of view of mode of operation, prostitutes may be categorized in three broad groups: those who work relatively independently, those who work through linkages with a variety of operators, and those who fall under the control of organized and stratified institutions. This categorization, however, is flexible in the sense that a

TABLE 4.6   Hospitality Girls in Manila given Health Certificates

Year	Number
1976	1,699
1977	2,039
1978	1,973
1979	2,685
1980	3,500

SOURCE: City Health Office, Manila City Hall.

prostitute may simultaneously fall under more than one group when dealing with different customers, or her practice may be controlled by different structures of the profession in different periods of her career.

The relatively independent operators include the sophisticated well-clad call girl who directly approaches clients in fashionable hotels or classy night clubs; the bar girl, waitress or entertainer who, while not being a full-time prostitute, supplements her income through occasional deals; and the ordinary heavily-made-up street-walker of the red light districts.

However, most prostitutes are dependent on a series of contacts for the maintenance of their practice and the procurement of clients. These intermediaries – specialized pimps, club owners, local guides, foreign tour guides, taxi drivers, and hotel personnel – take considerable proportions of the fees. According to a recent report,[16] some prostitutes in Manila earn less than 10 per cent of the fees paid by clients. The same report states that a number of hotels are substantively increasing their income from the joiner system. In Bangkok, the Grace Hotel is famous for catering to the sexual demands of Arab clients. The Hotel has become the place where the women gather daily and bargain their prices with the clients. The Hotel gets a percentage of this.

Military camps and naval bases are fertile areas for the emergence of a specialized system of prostitution. Countries of the region that have at some time in their history hosted foreign military bases are particular targets of sex tourism. It has been established that during 1962 to 1976, up to 50,000 American military personnel were stationed in different parts of Thailand and an average of 700,000 flew each year into the country for 'R & R' (rest and recreation). In response to the needs of these men, a network of sex entertainment of various types sprang up.

A study of the R and R industry in Olongapo City, the Philippines,[17] points out that the club girls receive no salary or benefits and depend on the 50 per cent commission on 'ladies drinks'. If a man desires to take a girl out of the bar, he pays a fee which is entirely kept by the bar owner, and the girl further negotiates a price with the customer.

In recent years there are changes in the structure of demand in sexual servicing. Traditionally this was linked to lone male professions like sailors and military. Presently, however, new complexes have grown to service businessmen as women are offerred as part of business deals and company bonus. Some tourist complexes even provide sex-tours as motivation for travel. These trends have led to an increase in the trade in female sexuality internationally.

Many examples of organized prostitution are found in the abundant and often expensively decorated massage parlours of Bangkok. Business transactions in those establishments are usually done at the counter where the display of a wide variety of numbered girls is presented to the clients through one-way windows. Pimps are not directly involved and the parlours offer the girls a safer and more comfortable environment than other forms of more loosely organized prostitution. In some of the establishments that cater to foreigners and high-income local customers accommodation and regular medical checks are available to the girls.

Currently under the disguise of marriage arrangements and the offer of good jobs abroad, many young women from Thailand and the Philippines are sent abroad only to find themselves trapped into prostitution and related services. Many sign contracts in languages they cannot read.

Clearly there are a number of different complexes that trade in female sexuality, some are traditional forms catering to local demands and some are of more recent origins serving mainly foreigners. The range includes massage parlours, a-go-go bars, sex clubs (where live shows are performed), brothels, semi-hotel/semi-brothels, and private apartments.

In one such massage parlour I visited, the Chao Phaya, in Bangkok, the girls sit behind the one-way mirror in different groups according to the kinds of things they can be expected to do and according to the cost of the transaction. One group only do massages (they earn the least), another group do massages but male clients may negotiate with the girls during the massage. Another group sits outside of the one-way mirror and this group provide solely sexual servicing (they earn the most). The massage parlour takes all the earnings of the girl during her first hour with every customer (about 300 – 500 bahts). The money she earns after that belongs to her after a small percentage is taken by the parlour. Parlours of this sort have become so profitable that banks readily give loans for their establishment. There are also many examples of restaurants not being successful until they convert themselves into massage parlours. Both local and foreign men frequent such places.

In Bangkok, places that cater mainly to tourists are Patpong I and Patpong II. There are over 50 bars along these two lanes. Many of them are a-go-go bars designed for foreign men particularly Germans, Japanese, American and Australian. The bars have names such as Rififi, Texas (where the decoration is completely Texan), Safari, Kings. There are also many homosexual bars and a lane of mainly Japanese bars where entry is based on memberships. Many of these bars are in fact owned and/or managed by foreigners. The girls employed by the bars are paid a small basic wage that varies according to whether they are mainly waitresses, a-go-go dancers or those who are involved in 'live-shows'. They get a percentage of all the drinks that they can get the customers to buy for them. Those who are willing to go out with customers earn more than those who do not. Those who are willing to do 'live-shows' which often involve lesbian acts, or acts that force the girls to use their bodies in distorted ways, earn more than others. On an average the a-go-go dancers take home about 2,500 bahts a month if they do not go out with customers. If they combine dancing with sexual servicing they may take home about 5,000 bahts.

The trade in female sexuality has become so much a part of Bangkok that some male officials of even the United Nations bring seminar participants to these places as part of their 'entertainment'.

The most vulnerable group who fall under the control of institutionalized prostitution are very young girls who are often coerced into the business. The following sections look at the specific problems faced by these young girls and some of the factors underlying the traffic in young women in the prostitution business. It is only by examining both these aspects that any realistic recommendations can be made for the protection and betterment of vulnerable groups of young women.

The Vulnerable Groups in Prostitution

Child labour and child prostitution exist in a number of South-East Asian countries, especially in the poorer parts of the region. According to a 1975 United Nations estimate, there were almost 42 million children under the age of 15 working in South and South-East Asian nations. In the South-East Asian region, it has been estimated that in some countries like Pakistan and Thailand more than 2 million children under 16 years of age work in small-scale factories, many of which are unlicensed.[18] In the cities of India, especially Bombay and Calcutta, one quarter of the children start work between the ages of 6 and 9 and nearly half between 10 and 12. Many young persons are sold into brothels.

In South-East Asia, it is believed that many of the young girls who are coerced into prostitution in the urban areas come from the rural poverty-stricken areas. Some agents offering work in the city are accused of buying rural children as young as 10 years old from their parents for low amounts. A substantial proportion of these children end up in the informal sector, selling newspapers and flowers amid the city traffic. There is some flow of personnel between the child labour market and the brothels which recruit young persons. A considerable number of young persons in the child labour market work under hazardous conditions. Some of the factories employ girls as young as 8 years to work from 6 a.m. to 8 p.m. without proper meals or overtime pay. They are forced to sit cross-legged for long periods. Many suffer from malnutrition and are provided with poor living quarters. Recently it was reported that in a confectionery factory in Thon Buri, Thailand, which employed 64 young girls about 8 to 10 years old to wrap sweets, two girls died, four were crippled as the result of their employment. The owner was brought before the Bangkok Military Court and jailed for four years and three months (see *Bangkok Post*, 20 October 1983). Under such conditions, it is easy to make these young persons believe that life is easier in the prostitution trade, where the person does not 'really work' but 'entertains'. The brothels are always on a look out for young virgin girls and pay a relatively high price for them. Many young girls after the loss of their virginity are forced to undergo operations to restore their hymens so that they may become 'virgins' once more.

Although a very substantial proportion of young girls enter the urban areas supposedly for the domestic labour market, many are sold to the brothels, where they work as domestic help until puberty. Often they come under the strict control of the secret societies which were involved in their migration to the city.[19] Because these young girls are sold or pawned, they are virtually slave prostitutes owned by the brothel-keepers, who keep them within the brothels and determine all their conditions of work. The girls' entire earnings are appropriated by their keepers and usually payments are made directly by the clients to the keepers. The women receive only the bare necessities of food and lodging. Unlike the sold prostitutes, the pawned prostitutes, however, have the hope of being 'free' once they have worked off a debt on behalf of their parents or guardians. Nevertheless, this 'freedom' is often an unrealized dream as the girls are in the control of the secret groups.

In Thailand, a document prepared in 1976 by the National Council of Social Welfare entitled 'Problems Concerning Prostitution and Trafficking in Women'[20] states that 'girls as young as 13 or 14 are brought from the provinces and sold into brothels, where they are imprisoned and greatly mistreated by pimps and operators'. Studies done on these young girls by the Council indicated that girls kept in brothels are usually the young ones between 13 and 16 years of age.

A study of prostitution in the Kramat Tunggak area in North Jakarta, done by members of the Jakarta Social Science Research Training Station (Pusat Latihan Penelitan Ilmu-ilmu Sosial Jakarta) in 1978[21] found that most of the young women they interviewed were migrants from West and Central Java. Almost half of the sample were in their teens and had no schooling experience. They gave various reasons for entering prostitution but the two common reasons are the difficulty in obtaining employment and the low wages offered to young women without any education. By entering prostitution they had hoped to earn 'easy money' but this expectation did not materialize for most of them. They found that after paying the pimps, their rent, dresses, cosmetics and medicine there is little left for themselves. This study found that many young women in prostitution eat only one decent meal a day and some are forced to sell their babies because of financial difficulty.

Many of the young girls who try to leave the prostitution trade and those who are 'rescued' from the brothels by social welfare departments in various countries are found to return after some time. The main reasons for the return may be the traditional approach to rehabilitation and the nature of training received at the rehabilitation centres set up in countries of the South-East Asian region for the 'moral re-education' and 'retraining' of the young girls. Little tends to be done to improve the self-concept of these young women. A general approach to rehabilitation is to train the girls to be domestic servants. As servants they earn low wages, are not protected by labour laws, work long hours with hardly a day off and are often subjected to scolding and ill-treatment. Hence, those with a background in prostitution tend to be attracted by the massage parlours and night-clubs.

The selling of young girls is not a new phenomenon in South-East Asia. There has been a historical link between domestic service and prostitution in the region as the following example will indicate.

Domestic Service and Prostitution – The Mui Tsai System[22]
Openly, the traffic in women and girls between Southern China and Malaya in the 1930s was for the purposes of domestic service. The Mui Tsai System is one where young girls sometimes below 10 years of age from impoverished families were sold or

adopted for their domestic services. During this period in the history of Malaya and Singapore, there was a shortage of women for household functions. Wealthy households would buy or adopt a mui tsai for her domestic help. Wages were rarely paid, but food, clothing and shelter were provided. When she grew up, the mui tsai was married to a man of her employer's choice and usually remained in domestic servitude to the household. Frequently the mui tsai became a concubine of a male member of the household. In 1934, almost 3,000 mui tsai were recorded in Malaya (including Singapore).

It is believed that the position of the mui tsai in Malaya was more vulnerable to exploitation and ill-treatment than in China. In the latter country, the parents and relatives of the mui tsai were in closer proximity and could keep some surveillance over her welfare. In Malaya, the distance and isolation of the mui tsai made it difficult to detect practices of ill-treatment. In the minority report of the Commission of inquiry into the mui tsai system in Malaya it was estimated that about 60 per cent of the mui tsai were ill-treated, beaten and scolded. Ill-treatment came in the form of bodily harm as well as overwork.

Although the young girls entered Malaya supposed for the domestic labour market, many mui tsai were sold to the brothels. Often they came under the strict control of the secret societies which were involved in their importation into Malaya and Singapore. In 1863 alone, 500 young girls were coerced from China by secret societies and their price on the Singapore market ranged from M$400. These girls were between the ages of 13 and 16. These young girls were meant not only for the brothels in Singapore but were also distributed to the mining and other commercial towns in Malaya, and other parts of South-East Asia.

Today the Mui Tsai System has been eradicated in Malaysia and Singapore and it is easy to dismiss it as an historical example and one extreme form of female child prostitution. However, in many present-day societies some variations of the mui tsai system still operate and the problems and control faced by the young girls are not too different in essence from this classical historical case. Useful lessons and methodology could be drawn from a detailed study of the conditions and of the struggle that led to the abolition of the Mui Tsai System.

The Social Context of Prostitution

To understand the traffic in young women, it is necessary to examine the economic situation with which the young women and their parental households are located, as well as the social and cultural conditions which push young women into the sexual trade. Four factors may be identified and these factors are discussed below:

Poverty and prostitution. In many rural societies and urban groups in poverty, child work is part of the process of socialization and the child is incorporated into working life between the ages of 5 and 15. The distinctions between childhood and adulthood as well as between the economic and the non-economic are not as well defined as in the case of the better-off classes. While artisan and agricultural skills are passed from one generation to the next through the gradual incorporation of the child in household subsistence activities, the child may also be exposed to exploitation between generations and between social groups. One of the most extreme form of child exploitation occurs among groups faced with poverty and consequent indebtedness; in such cases, it is common practice to pledge children as workers as part of a debt payment. Which child is eventually chosen to be sold off or bonded depends on the demand in the child labour market and also the supply factors within the household. Both males and female children have been found in bonded labour. However, when a female child is selected for sale or bondage, she is often given into domestic service or prostitution, unlike the male child who is often found in unskilled agricultural work, small-scale or urban commodity production. It is only recently that reports have emerged indicating the use of young boys in homosexual prostitution in the Philippines, in Thailand and in Malaysia.

The social-cultural values and prostitution. It is now accepted in sociology and anthropology that personality development, role acceptance and the internalization of social norms are transmitted in a way that reflects and perpetuates the existing classification system of the larger society of which the individual is a member. Certain social and cultural values, particularly those related to virginity, sometimes act as 'push factors'. For young women in many Asian societies, the loss of virginity even through rape means that they are socially stigmatized. Even though violence has been used on them, they are regarded as 'spoilt' women, not quite 'proper' women. There is social pressure to make the women believe that 'once they are spoilt', they are 'spoilt for life'. When this classification system exists in a situation of few employment alternatives for women together with family pressure for financial support, the young women easily turn to prostitution as an income-earning opportunity especially since they themselves believe that they are 'already spoilt' and there are few ways in which they can change their 'bad history'.[23]

The violence and coercive structures which surround the prostitution business make it difficult for young women to leave the trade once they are coerced into it. The control by gangsters and the punishment they inflict on the women often deter young women from leaving. In Bangkok, there have been press reports on how physical intimidation by brothel operators and the collusion between the police and brothel operators has forced the girls who had escaped back into the prostitution trade. (See *The Nation*, 10 February 1982.)

Ideology of male sexual needs. One of the main reasons why prostitution has been a thriving business is the ideology of male sexual needs and the double standard of sexual morality. This ideology holds that there are differences between female and male sexuality. While the females are usually passive and responsive to male initiatives, the males have strong sexual urges that need satisfaction. In their socialization process, males are provided with the 'macho' image of 'the man'. Proper males are expected to be sexually virile while proper women are expected to be docile and repressed in her sexuality. Also, women are often trained to emphasize affection rather than sex. Because the sexual 'demand' is socially defined as natural for men and less natural for proper women, in a male-dominated society, it brings with it the right of males to sexual servicing outside of the household. In contrast, the 'proper' woman is one who limits sex to her marriage relationship. Hence a category of socially ostracized women exist whose purpose is to meet male sexual demands – the prostitutes. Prostitution as a practice hence embodies the structures of male dominance.

Conclusion: Strategies to Deal with Vulnerable Groups in Prostitution

Prostitution is a response to several problems in society. In the attempt to improve the situation of young women in prostitution there must be less sensationalism in defining the problem areas, and a more accurate identification of 'the problem group(s)'. The issue of who or what is 'the problem group' is in fact more complex and may affect some of the basic structures of how society is presently organized. From the above discussion, 'the problem groups' appear to be the following:

1. The adult male who feels that he has the right of sexual access to even very young persons if he can pay for their services;
2. The groups associated with the traffic in young women – the pimps, the gangsters, the corrupt officials, bar owners, employees of the lodging and entertainment facilities;
3. The parents who for one reason or another sold the child into the trade;
4. Members of society by whom such abuse of young persons is ignored and sometimes tolerated or considered a normal solution to the poverty problem of marginal groups;
5. People in power positions who actively maintain the skewed distribution of resources in society so that many can exist only by resorting to practices such as the bondage or selling of children.

Past attempts to deal with the issue have called for the elimination of prostitution. In Pakistan, for example, the death penalty for prostitution has recently been proposed by an official committee.[24] Other countries have taken up the issue more leniently through conscious tolerance or a complete negligence. As it stands, consciousness raising, moralizing campaigns and imposition of legal constraints have been of limited value. Such resistance to change is partly because those movements have tended to behave in a moralistic and simplistic manner, partly because of wide discrepancies between law and implementation, and most importantly because prostitution is enmeshed with sexuality, one of the most basic human drives.

It is difficult to bring out concrete strategies on controversial issues, especially when the incendiary ground is culture-bound sexual morality for which there are no universal hard and fast rules. It seems necessary, however, to concentrate efforts on correcting those instances where the power imbalance among buyer, middleman and supplier results in violence, degradation and other violations of human dignity. Special consideration must be given to the use of coercion and deception by which young women are led into prostitution through entrapments; the use of force and violence by which women are forced to engage in sexual perversions; the selling of young girls by parents and the capitalization on female virginity; and the exploitation of the prostitution of others by pimps, club owners, hotel personnel, tourist agents and members of international syndicates.

There is certainly a need for careful research and policy planning at both the macro- and micro-levels; and most importantly, a need for serious restructuring of the organizational and ideological relationships in which different groups of men and women are engaged.

Notes and References

1. Ron O'Grady, (ed.), 1980, Third World Tourism, Christian Conference of Asia, Report of a Workshop on Tourism, Manila.
2. A variety of books have been written on the economic advantages of tourism, e.g., Peter Michael, 1969, *International Tourism: The Economics and Development of the International Tourist Trade*, Hutchinson, London; Harry Clement, 1961, *The Future of Tourism in the Pacific and the Far East*, U.S. Department of Commerce, Washington; A.J. Burkart and S. Medlik, (eds), 1975, *The Management of Tourism*, Heinemann, London.
3. Quoted by: Kin Thisa, 1980, *Providence and Prostitution: Image and Reality for Women in Buddhist Thailand*, Change International Reports: Women and Society, Calvert's North Star Press, London, p. 14. Jane Cottingham, 1981, 'Sex Included', *Development Forum*, June.
4. A concrete example of such practice is brought up by Anne L. Blasing, 1982, in her paper on 'Prostitution Tourism from Japan and other Asian Countries', Presented to the first Asian Consultation of Trafficking in Women, Manila.
5. Dean Barret, 1980, *The Girls of Thailand*, Toppan Printing Co., Hong Kong, pp. 108–113.
6. Estimates within the range are found in: Pasuk Phongpaichit, 1980, 'Rural Women of Thailand: From Peasant Girls to Bangkok Masseuses'. International Labour Office. World Employment Programme Research. Tourism and Prostitution. ISIS International Bulletin No. 13, Geneva, 1979. Dithakar Bhakdi, 1976, 'Problems concerning prostitution and trafficking in women in Thailand'. National Council for Social Welfare.
7. Pasuk Phongpaichit, op. cit.
8. Leo Van Der Velden, 1981, 'Visitors and tourists to Thailand and their eventual demand for prostitution'. Unpublished paper. Accuracy of this figure may be questioned on grounds that it is based on male tourists who officially state in immigration cards that they travel for 'holiday' and exclude those who travel for 'business' and furthermore it assumes that the number of female tourists 'neutralize' the same number of male tourists, and that the girls make an average of four contacts per week.
9. Thepanom Muangman *et al.*, 1980, Report of a study on education, attitude and work of 1,000 massage girls in Bangkok with special reference to family planning, pregnancy, abortion, venereal disease and drug addiction (unpublished paper in Thai, Bangkok).
10. Brief Report on the Situation of Masseuse Attendants, Hostesses and Hospitality Girls in Manila. Presented at the First Asian Consultation on Trafficking of Women, Manila, 12–15 March 1982.
11. Statistics on Women and Development, Women's Bureau of Sri Lanka, Ministry of Plan

Implementation, 15 May 1981.

12. Discussed by the psychologist Albert Ellis in his analysis of H. Benjamin's paper 'Prostitution Reassessed', International Journal of Sexology, August 1951. Also discussed in H. Benjamin and R.E.L. Masters, 1965, *Prostitution and Morality*, Souvenir Press, London.

13. Since this paper is focused on women, and given the greater incidence of prostitution among females, reference is only made to female prostitution.

14. Pasuk Phongpaichit, op. cit.

15. Sudarat Serrewat, 1983, 'Prostitution: Thai – European Connection', A Summary Report, World Council of Churches, Geneva, July.

16. Lin Newman, 1982, 'Shadows of Pleasure', Presented at the First Asian Consultation on Trafficking of Women, Manila.

17. Leopoldo Moselina, 1978, 'Olongapo's R and R Industry: A Sociological Analysis of Institutionalized Prostitution', Unpublished Master Thesis.

18. Economic and Social Commission for Asia and the Pacific, 1981, *Economic and Social Survey of Asia and the Pacific*.

19. Some of the information here is based on interviews with local researchers, also a variety of reports that have regularly appeared in the local press and personal observations.

20. S. Dithakar Bhakdi, 1976, 'Problems Concerning Prostitution and Trafficking in Women in Thailand'. The National Council of Social Welfare, Thailand.

21. See, Ibrahim Amali, 1978, 'Young Women in Prostitution', Report prepared by the Jakarta Social Science Research Station.

22. Most of the information here is based on the Report of the Commission on Mui Tsai in W. Woods, 1937, *Mui Tsai in Hong Kong and Malaya*, Colonial Office, London, and on B. Lasker, 1972, *Human Bondage in South-East Asia*, Greenwood Press, Connecticut.

23. This finding is confirmed by observations made by some officers in the UNHCR when referring to prostitution among refugee girls.

24. 'Drive to Clean Up Pakistan, Prostitutes May Face Execution', 1982, *The Bangkok Post*, 18 October, p. 6.

CHAPTER 5

Women in the Plantation Sector

Introduction

The plantation sector has been one of the chief means by which several countries in South-East Asia, particularly Malaysia, Indonesia and the Philippines have been integrated as peripheries to the world market system. The present chapter is concerned with the conditions of women, mainly family rubber estate workers in Peninsular Malaysia. Currently the rubber estate sector in Malaysia is undergoing major changes with a very significant restructuring of women's role.

Women workers in the rubber estates have so far been totally overlooked by researchers and policy-makers, although they form over 50 per cent of the labour force. This neglect may have come about, firstly because of certain state policies that have resulted in Tamil workers generally being given low priority status because of their ethnicity and secondly, because the family-group work as a production unit on most estates. On the plantation, the man, as head of the household, is paid for his job plus the work done by his wife and children. Moreover, research priorities are focused on technological improvement in latex extraction and the development of high-yield rubber trees rather than on the women and men engaged in rubber production, who have not been a priority concern. This is so even though rubber is one of the three main raw materials (the other two being tin and palm oil) on which the Malaysian economy depends.

Women's subordinate position on the rubber estates must be examined within the structure of production and the labour process on the plantation. The starting point of this chapter is that women's position on the plantations cannot be seen in isolation but must be placed within the following contexts:

1. fluctuating market prospects for natural rubber as a commodity on the international market both in the colonial period and at the present-day;
2. the organization of production and class hierarchy within the plantation: internal patterns of economic and social organization set the constraints within which the estate labourers must operate;
3. the nature of the household's incorporation into the plantation economy.

This chapter consists of three parts. The first section is an historical account of the plantation system. The way the problems of the rubber estates present themselves today remains inextricably bound with the dynamics of the plantation system during the colonial period. The organization of the estate system, the economic and social relationships and nature of the workforce were all set up during this period and have remained in their essential elements to the present day.

The second section analyses some new present-day estate systems within the current global context, looking at the pressure of competition generated by the technological development of synthetic rubber, the falling demand for natural rubber on the world market, the recent recovery of natural rubber as a commodity, and the diversification of international capital in Malaysia. These changes have caused the increasing displacement, relocation and re-organization of male and female labour, although in different ways.

The final part of the study explores, through the use of a case study, what these changes mean for women estate workers and their households. By examining women's labour in this way a picture of the changing utilization of female labour over time may be seen.

The Colonial Period and the Plantation Workers

During the colonial period, the rubber plantations became a means through which Malaya was integrated as a periphery into the world capitalist system. The estates operated in an extremely profitable environment in terms of capital and labour. Land was made available by the colonial government to estates on very liberal terms. Rent was only ten cents per acre for the first ten years, after which the rent was fifty cents per acre.[1] Most European companies were formed outside Malaya (mainly in London) and ownership was separated from management by great distance. An important intermediate organization between the directors and managers was the agency house.[2] The largest of them managed many different companies, and often they would own shares in these companies. In the 1930s, the four largest agency houses managed or controlled more than one-third of all European-owned estate acreage in Malaya. This, together with a tendency to interlocking directorships, gave unity to an industry which otherwise was fragmented. The agency houses also played an important role in raising capital for the companies formed after 1910.

The Plantation Workforce
With the rapid spread of rubber estates, there was the problem of obtaining a regular supply of cheap and disciplined labour to ensure the continued profitability of the estates. The Malays were far too few for this purpose. Moreover, they were reluctant to accept estate work.[3] The planters were forced to import labour from India, particularly from the famine prone areas of South India.

Ethnicity as a Strategy in Labour Recruitment. Most of the work on the estate was monotonous and had to be done by hand. The South Indian peasants, particularly the so-called untouchables or low-cast Madrasi, were recruited.[4] It was said that these people were easily manageable, worked well under supervision, and were most amenable to the lowly-paid and regimented life of the estates. In short, they were 'a peaceable and easily governed race'.[5] Also, Tamil labour was desired to offset the growing numbers of Chinese workers who, with their organizations, provided a certain amount of political resistance at the workplace and hence proved less manageable. The Governor of the Straits Settlements, in his despatch to the Secretary of State, stated:

> I am also anxious for political reasons that the great preponderance of the Chinese over any other race in these settlements, and to a less marked degree in some of the Native States under our administration should be counterbalanced as much as possible by the influx of Indians and other nationalities.[6]

Additionally, as India was a British colony, immigration could be arranged to meet labour demand quickly. From 1900 to 1931, arrivals from India averaged 80,000 a year.

The recruitment of Tamil workers was done through the 'Kangany System'. The kangany was usually a recruiter from a slightly higher caste who had control over groups of labourers. Under this system, a kangany was sent by an estate to obtain labourers in India. They would frequently recruit family units from the same village and hence groups who had some social ties to maintain. In Malaya, the kangany was the key figure in the control and management of the workers as he was the contact point between the estate management and the workers, and had great power over the lives of the workers. The workers were placed in groups which in turn had a group leader. Organizationally, life on the estate was built on very hierarchical and feudal principles with authority and power structures instilled and reinforced at every level of working life. This work hierarchy was further reinforced by the caste system. Although all the workers were from the low caste, there were people from certain sub-castes who considered themselves superior. This view of human relationships was given additional support through recruitment policy and work organization of the estate which drew the kangany and the group leaders from the higher sub-castes.

From Male Workers to Family Units. For over three decades the bulk of the labour recruited for plantation work was male. It was only in 1928 that the 'sex-ratio rule' of the Indian Emigration Act of 1922 was enforced in Malaya. This rule required that for every three males allowed to emigrate, two females must also be assisted to emigrate. Attempts were made to foster 'family formation' and to develop family life among the labourers through the allocation of very low quality barrack-like houses on the estates.

This change in the labour recruitment policy did not conflict with the interests of the plantation in Malaya, as it helped in the creation of a permanent and steady workforce that could reproduce itself during what was a highly active phase in capital accumulation. Male workers who were initially recruited could not act as a force towards a permanent supply of labour in the way family units could. For a long while the male workers were tied to the estates as indentured labour. After serving out their term of indenture, these male workers became 'free labourers'. Although the term 'free labourer' had little real meaning on a particular estate, since there was no difference in working conditions between a 'free labourer' and an indentured labourer, the former could sell his labour to the estate of his choice. In other words, he was potentially mobile.

The family units recruited were less mobile. They were expected to repay the estate all the costs of their journey out of their wages and hence were in constant debt-bondage. As family housing was tied to estate employment, it became increasingly difficult to look for alternative jobs that could maintain family subsistence and reproduction. On the estate, the labour-intensive method of tapping and weeding lent itself to full family participation, and a certain amount of subsistence crops like tapioca could be grown on available land near the barracks.

Also with the recruitment of family units, the preservation of caste identity was made easier as there were more opportunities to act out these relationships. Caste differences were expressed in the allocation of living quarters, in religious festivals and through the choosing of marriage partners. The ideology behind the caste system was useful in the control of workers and in the maintenance of the kangany's social position.

Women as Casual Tappers and Unskilled Workers. There is no material that focuses specifically on women plantation workers during the colonial period. Some data, however, does exist on wage policy towards female estate labour.

The dynamics of a plantation economy are essentially capital accumulation. In a situation where the level of technology is minimal and labour is regarded as the major production cost, in order to obtain the maximum in surplus value, there can be a lowering of the value of labour power through the reduction of the real wage and/or an increase in the intensity of work. The use of women and children as lower-paid or unpaid labour becomes a strategy to lower the value of labour to capital and therefore raise the relative rate of surplus value or profit level.

In the plantations, women work as rubber tappers and field workers. As tappers, they do the same jobs as men, tapping the rubber tree, collecting the latex and bringing it to the collection centre. The field workers are almost all women and children, dependents of the male rubber tappers. They are employed in miscellaneous jobs of estate maintenance, chiefly in weeding. Generally, rubber tapping is regarded as skilled work while fieldwork is considered as unskilled.

Table 5.1 provides an idea of the historical discrimination in wages by sex for different areas in Malaya. Plantations in Malaya were divided into two types of areas: the easily accessible areas with a fairly healthy environment, where the cost of living was lower (Type A), e.g. Province Wellesley, Malacca, and most of the Federated Malay States. The second type were the less accessible and unhealthy areas where malaria was widespread (Type B).

Besides discrimination in wage rates, a sexual division also operated by status of employment. The majority of male rubber tappers were employed as full-time workers on the *check-roll system*, and they received a fixed daily wage for a whole day's work (9 hours). The majority of women rubber tappers were regarded as casual

TABLE 5.1   Discrimination in Wages by Sex (Malaya)

Year	District	Full-day's wages in cents	
		Male	*Female*
1924	Selangor (A)	35	27
1925	Selangor (A)	40	30
1927	Province Wellesley (A)	50	40
1927	Pahang (B)	58	46
1929	Kelantan (B)	58	46
1930	Province Wellesley (A)	40	32
1930	Kelantan (B)	47	37

SOURCE: Bauer, 1960, pp. 181–82.

workers and were employed under the *task system* and the *result system*. Those under the task system were assigned a certain amount of work and paid by the number of tasks completed per month. The wages of this category of workers fluctuated depending on the amount of available work in any one month. Workers employed under the *result system* were also given tasks but were paid according to the weight of dry rubber contained in the latex obtained from tapping. Wages not only fluctuated according to the availability of work on the plantations, but also according to factors such as the terrain, distance of the plantation, and the height of the tapping cut on the trees. Both the task system and the result system of employment were means of circumventing payment of standard wage rates which were already low.[7]

The bulk of the women workers on the plantation during this period, however, were not tappers but were employed as field workers. As field workers, their wages were even lower than casual tappers. These women were almost always dependents of the male rubber tappers.

'. . . the tapper's wages were not adequate to cover his dependents' cost of living. . . . Either the tapper had to be paid enough to support his dependents or the dependents had to be employed. The latter course was cheaper.'[8]

There was an added reason for the employment of dependents as field workers. Being residents on the estate, the non-tapping labourers constituted a reserve tapping force needed to fill in absence among the workers, without being given the status of tappers.

'To reduce or do away with the non-tapping labour force would make maintenance of a full tapping force difficult. Every field must be kept in production; a day's wages saved by leaking latex in the tree due to a vacancy in the tapping force was not enough compensation for the revenue lost.'[9]

Socially, there was strong control over women in terms of her production and reproduction activities. The women were, together with the men, already isolated from the rest of the Malayan society on arrival. This isolation is not only geographical but also economic (in the sense that they were unable to find employment outside of the estate system) and political (in the sense that they were subject to the powers of the kangany and the whole estate system). However for the women, there was an additional side to the isolation based on their gender. Within Hinduism, the dominant religious system of the estate workers, women were considered inferior to men. With the new isolation, this inequality became more expressed in the daily lives of the people as women became totally dependent on their husbands for their existence.

Women, their Families and Unemployment. The conditions of the women plantation workers and their families were not static but were closely linked to the fluctuating market prospects for natural rubber as a commodity on the international market. During boom periods when there was an expansion of rubber production and a shortage of labour, attempts were made to make Malaya as attractive as possible for family units. Recommendations were made to provide schooling for labourers' children and maternity allowances for pregnant women. These recommendations were subsequently made the legal obligations of the employer.

In times of slump, unemployment affected the plantations. This was extremely severe during the outbreak of the First World War when the rubber price declined sharply due to international financial and market uncertainties. The transfer of funds from abroad was halted and the rubber market in London was temporarily closed. Employers began to discharge labourers and wages were cut. The women casual tappers and field workers were the first to be retrenched, followed by some male workers. The male workers who remained employed worked for lower wages. Many enterprises could carry on only by postponing financial obligations. Besides the reduced wages, numerous employers paid part wages in food, deferring the balance till later.[10]

Attempts were made to reduce the families' cost of living to meet the lower wages.[11] A lower price was put on opium, tobacco and toddy (alcohol made from coconut sap) as a substantial part of the worker's, particularly the male worker's, income was spent on these items. Alcoholism among male workers was prevalent.

The full effects of the depression were felt in 1921.

'These coolies (labourers) being out of work for long spells wandered about ill-fed and like helpless children sleeping anywhere on roadsides with the result that they became malarious and anaemic and when re-employed had to go to hospital to be reconditioned.'[12]

The Government's chief means of coping with growing unemployment was repatriation. At the same time, they were concerned that not too many labourers might leave Malaya that actual labour shortage would occur, as labour was needed to restore estate production when times improved. Most planters were willing to retain family units at reduced wages.

Employers reported that they were operating their estates on a 'three-quarter time basis'. The male head of the household worked three-quarters of a full day and was paid three-quarters of the standard wage rate of 40 cents. Widows would also be employed, but at a much lower rate, three-quarters of 30 cents.[13] Employers in many districts were paying less than standard wages. Wage-cutting was so bad that the

Government had to act to ensure that the part-time standard wage was kept. By June 1933, wages for male workers had fallen to 28 cents a day and those of female workers had fallen to 24 cents a day.[14]

Towards the end of 1936, rubber prices moved sharply upwards towards what became the peak price for rubber in the 1930s. Wages of workers were raised to 45 cents for men and 36 cents for women. With higher export quotas and improved rubber prices, there was a rising demand for labour and 1937 became the third largest year on record for Indian immigration. However, this boom began to fall off quickly and by May 1938 the prices reached a low of 5 pence as compared to the high of 1 shilling and 2 pence in the previous year. Workers' wages were once again reduced and the cuts were strengthened by the abundance of available labour.

The good – bad year movements did not restructure the position of women within the estate system although there was a breakdown of many traditional relationships and many women had to find new ways of supporting themselves. The notion of male superiority remained intact even with the growth of alcoholism and the use of violence on women during hard times. The lives of women were still dependent on the men and their needs. It was only with the struggle for independence and several changes on the international and national scene that new forces were introduced into the estate system with the promise of a better life for women, even if indirectly.

One such change is the social climate that resulted from the national struggle for political independence and which gave rise to the formation of workers' organization. Before the Second World War, there was an absence of a unified Indian working class organization on the estates. There were some small groups which attempted to alleviate labour conditions in the early days of colonialism through pressures for the payment of standard minimum wages, the allotment of land at one-sixth of an acre for garden cultivation and the inspection of vessels carrying Indian labourers. However these small groups remained amorphous and fragmented until the disruption and havoc that the depression brought to workers on the estates. A consolidated Indian semi-nationalism took root by the 1940s in the federation of a member of existing Indian associations. This federation turned its attention to problems concerning wages, housing and general working conditions among Indian workers.

The resulting opposition between colonized labour and colonial employers expressed itself in labour strikes among the estate workers. In May 1941, strikers were shot, causing a sense of revulsion among the Indian community. The legitimization for the shooting was the accusation that the federation was involved with the communists. In June 1948, a triple murder of estate planters marked the beginning of what has come to be known as the Communist Insurgency in Malaya. The 1950s saw the de-registration of several trade unions as a distinction was made by the government between 'genuine' and 'political' unions. The result of the Trade Union Act was the destruction of powerful unions and the proliferation of less powerful ones with the limited aim of resolving specific work grievances rather than attempting to change the economic and political structures on a national scale.

The growth of trade unionism on the estates brought a certain amount of change in the traditional superiority – inferiority relationships among the workers, as old standards and values were being questioned and protest grew against abuses by people in power. Although the trade union movement has succeeded in achieving better wages and housing for the workers in general, it has shown little concern for the special problems faced by women. Up to the present time, the trade union has been very highly male-dominated and the leadership usually taken by the men from the higher sub-castes. The mode of conflict resolution for the woman is still through her husband. The woman will speak to her husband who will sometimes take up her complaint. There is still a very strong feeling that women should not intrude into the affairs of men and trade unionism is regarded as one such sphere. Yet, trade unions are seen usually to represent *all* workers' interests. However, the rights of women workers are not conceived of in the same way as those of men in the minds of their male leaders.

The Rubber Plantations and their Workforce in the Present-day.

Intense Competition from Synthetic Rubber

The major difference between rubber production in the colonial period and the present-day period is the intense competition between Natural Rubber (NR) and Synthetic Rubber (SR). It was the Second World War which gave the main impetus to the development of SR on a large scale. Western Europe and the United States, cut off from their main sources of natural rubber, turned to the domestic chemical industry to meet their large and expanding need for elastomers.[15]

Synthetic rubber consumption rose from 20 per cent of the market in 1950 to nearly two-thirds in 1970. This was due to the rapid rise in the price of NR in the early 1950s; supplies being threatened as a result of the political conflict in NR-producing countries (Malaya, Indonesia and Ceylon); improved quality and processing of SR through technical advances; the low price of crude oil, the primary raw material of SR, in the 1950s and 1960s; and the US Government subsidizing the industry by selling SR production facilities to private companies in 1955 at 60 per cent of the replacement cost.[16]

With low oil prices up to the early 1970s, the challenge from SR was formidable. Compared with NR, SR is a machine-intensive product giving easier control over the production process. Rubber trees, however, take as long as seven years before maturity, and nine to sixteen years to reach optimum production. SR came to replace NR in North America more than anywhere else and NR is used there only where technically indispensable. The result was the dramatically falling market price for NR, particularly between 1955 and 1968. Currently, prices for NR have improved, particularly after 1973.

Losing its monopoly position in the world market, the NR industry saw itself in a situation of competition. Over a range of uses SR and NR could be substituted. NR, however, still remains the most versatile and balanced material, and no single synthetic has yet been devised which contains all the qualities of the natural product, though different synthetics may match or improve upon some of its properties.[17] In fact, it has been estimated that in about 25 – 30 per cent of the world rubber consumption, SR and NR cannot be substituted for each other. This leaves a market area of about 50 per cent open to competition.[18]

Changes Made by Estates in Response to Competition from SR

In Peninsular Malaysia, rubber is still the largest single crop by acreage. Out of 6.9 million acres under cultivation, 61 per cent are under rubber. The number of workers employed in the rubber estates and smallholdings account for 50 per cent of the 1.2 million employed in agriculture.

The growth in smallholder production is also related to the ways the estates have responded to the intense international competition from SR. First, old rubber trees have been burnt and rubber estates converted into palm oil estates. Secondly, foreign capital is no longer confining itself to the primary sector, but is taking an active role in manufacturing. Former rubber land has been bought and converted into industrial sites, Free Trade Zones, and New Towns.

Estates that continue with rubber production have developed ways of producing high quality rubber and ways of cutting labour cost. High yield, new rubber clones have been planted. By 1973, 95 per cent of the large estates that continued with rubber production had replanted and were using stimulants.[19] To keep labour costs low, estates under the control of the larger agency houses have begun to apply a change in the technology of latex extraction — the creation of the rotor injector. The aim of this instrument is to cut down the number of permanent workers needed on the plantation and hence keep labour costs at a minimum. This new tool breaks away from the traditional tapping knife and employs the puncture method to stimulate the flow of latex from the trees. According to the RRIM (Rubber Research Institute of Malaysia), tapping with this tool requires little skill; it is light to handle and is operated by four penlight batteries. A tapper could tap about 900 trees a day as compared to 350 – 400 trees at present. Sime Darby, the largest agency house (which has 23 companies controlling 56 rubber estates with a total of 294,115 acres of plantation), is talking at present of using this semi-automated tapping because of what it calls 'labour shortage on the estate'.[20] There have also been attempts in the 1980s to mechanise latex collection. These have so far been unsuccessful. The small estates, those outside the control of the agency houses, find that it is more profitable to convert themselves into smallholdings to reduce labour costs, and also to qualify for government aid given to smallholders in the form of the New Block Planting Scheme.

The Estate Workforce, 1967 – 1982

Labour force figures in Table 5.2 indicate a decreasing trend in the number of male workers on the rubber estates. In 1967, there were 114,470 male workers in this sector. However, by 1982, this figure had fallen to 63,702, that is by 44 per cent. Although in terms of absolute numbers the female workforce had decreased over these years, the percentage of female workers had increased. In 1967, women formed 47 per cent of the total workforce. By 1982, this percentage had increased to 57 per cent.

The decline in male workers in the rubber estates is linked to the decline in the demand for rubber in the commodity market especially during the 1975 – 82 period. The prolonged international recession, high stock levels of rubber in the producing countries, and declining global demand for automobiles and tyres had an adverse impact on rubber prices.

TABLE 5.2 Employment in Estates

Type of Estates	1967			1975			1980			1981			1982		
	Male	Female	Young Persons	Male	Female	Young Persons	Male	Female	Young Persons	Male	Female	Young Persons	Male	Female	Young Persons
Rubber	114,470	108,590	8,840	88,670	95,420	3,160	72,820	92,730	1,660	70,570	92,760	1,290	63,702	83,713	880
Coconut	2,710	1,900	120	1,850	1,510	90	1,920	1,770	20	1,684	1,602	20	2,210	2,150	18
Oil Palm	16,630	9,940	1,180	42,120	21,070	3,390	51,460	24,370	2,010	49,213	22,305	1,229	55,410	36,740	300
Tea	2,210	2,240	370	1,460	1,770	240	1,140	1,580	60	1,030	1,420	60	836	1,091	24
Pineapple	2,030	1,180	160	660	390	–	780	820	30	700	730	–	683	688	5

SOURCE: Ministry of Labour, Labour and Manpower Report, 1981/1982.

Many of the displaced male workers were being absorbed into the oil palm estates, especially since many rubber estates have been converted to oil palm cultivation. Male workers increased from 16,630 to 55,410 during the 1967–82 period in the oil palm sector. Female workers are also employed in this sector, but to a much smaller extent than in the rubber estates.

Wages of employees, especially of rubber tappers, in the rubber estates are subject to fluctuations as a result of the price of rubber on the world market as shown in Table 5.3.

TABLE 5.3   Wages in the Rubber Estates 1973–1982 (Average earnings)

Year	Mandores/ Kepala (Males)	Rubber Tappers (Males & Females)	Weeders (Males & Females)	Arsenite Sprayers (Males & Females)	Factory Workers (Males & Females)	Total Number of Workers
1973	165	149	77	111	113	191,760
1974	201	195	100	121	136	193,160
1975	191	139	92	121	132	187,250
1976	230	212	126	160	178	178,930
1977	201	197	120	164	161	174,900
1978	243	220	127	154	179	177,270
1979	261	254	146	145	207	170,670
1980	300	259	169	224	225	167,210
1981	331	266	171	224	234	164,620
1982	340	267	188	253	302	148,294

SOURCE: Ministry of Labour, Government of Malaysia.

The highest paid workers are the Mandores who supervise the manual workers in the plantation. They are all males. The lowest paid are the weeders who are mainly women. The average earnings of rubber tappers which stood at $149.00 in 1973 has increased to $267.00 in 1982. The earning differentials between rubber tappers and weeders which was 93 per cent in 1973 has been reduced to 30 per cent in 1980 as more and more women were employed as tappers. The differentials between rubber tappers and weeders can be explained by the fact that tapping is considered an act that requires a considerable degree of skill. The exercise of this skill is important to obtain maximum latex from the tree with minimum bark consumption. In contrast, weeding work is said not to involve much skill. In 1982 Mandores earned an average of $340.00. Factory workers in the estates earned $113.00 in 1973 and $302.00 in 1982. The higher earning is due to the influence of the recently concluded collective agreement for factory workers in 1982.

Since 1959, the take-home wage of rubber workers has been made up of a guaranteed basic wage and an output factor for latex above a basic poundage and for scrap rubber. This collective wage agreement was made between the then Malayan Planting Industries' Employers' Association (MPIEA)[21] – the main employer organization in the industry – and the National Union of Plantation Workers (NUPW), the sole workers' union on plantations and the largest employees' trade union in the country representing 50 per cent of the rubber estate workforce. Prior to this agreement, the wages of tappers and field workers fluctuated with the price of rubber, the task size and the retail price index. This agreement has been revised several times with slight upward revisions in the rate of basic pay.

The basic wage rates and incentive payments for tappers and field workers for 1975, 1976 and 1979 are given in the MAPA circulars reproduced in Appendix I to show in detail how wages are calculated. The basic daily wage for able-bodied males working as field workers was M$3.20 in 1975. For female able-bodied field workers, the rate was M$2.75. Rubber tappers have been given equal pay since 1953.[22] This equality in pay did not spread to the field workers until 1976. By 1979, both male and female field workers earned M$3.60 in basic daily wages.

Even with the introduction of the incentive system, and of equal pay, the wages of large numbers of rubber tappers remain low and unsteady. According to the *Third Malaysia Plan 1976–1980*, there were about 250,000 estate workers in 148,400 households in 1970. The estimated percentage of households said to be in poverty[23] was 40 per cent, as shown in Table 5.4 These households were mainly single wage-earner families (or with two wage-earners in the case of large families). By 1975, the percentage of households in poverty increased to 47 per cent, although the number of poor households remained almost constant. This is due to a reduction in the total number of households engaged in rubber production as the result of the reorganization of the plantations.

TABLE 5.4   Rubber Estate Households in Poverty

Year	Total Households ('000)	Total Poor Households ('000)	Percentage of Poor Households
1970	148.4	59.4	40.1
1975	127.0	59.7	47.0

SOURCE: Government of Malaysia, Third Malaysia Plan, 1976–1980, p. 163.

This percentage is slightly higher than the 1975 national estimate – 43 per cent – of households living below the poverty line. There is little doubt that estate workers form one of the largest groups living in poverty. However, they are not at the lowest level of poverty when compared to other rural poverty groups. The two largest poverty groups are the landless paddy farmers and the rural rubber smallholders. One study found that 60 per cent of rubber smallholders live below the poverty line.[24]

Nonetheless, the causes of the poverty of estate workers need examination, and may be linked to three factors (1) the task size (2) the computation of the fair wage for estate workers, and (3) retrenchment and subsequent unemployment of estate workers. The task size affects the workers' take-home pay: 'it depends on the length of the cut, the position of the cut, the yield of the tree (i.e., high yield or low yield), and the nature of the terrain. On flat terrain, and cuts involving low half-spiral systems, a worker can tap as many as 600 trees in one morning. When the terrain is hilly and ladder tapping is necessary because of the height of the cuts, the number is reduced to about 300. The incentive payments for workers allocated the latter areas are very low because of the difficulty of the tasks. These payments are further affected by whether the worker has been assigned the low-yield or high-yield trees.

The take-home pay also varies according to seasonality, reaching a low of M$80 in the rainy months (January – March) and a high of M$160 in June to July (based on an interview with some tappers and checked with estate community officer). In the 1976 MAPA – NUPW Agreement, it has been agreed that on washout days, i.e., when tappers have already started tapping but are prevented by rain from completing their normal duties during the working hours, the day is treated as a working day and the tappers are allowed their basic wage and incentive bonus. When late tapping is carried out because of the rain, the incentive rate is increased by 3 cents in the low-yielding areas and 2 cents in the high-yielding fields. Because of all these factors, in order to have a living wage for the household, not only the man but also his wife and children have to be put out to work.

A Case Study of Women Plantation Workers

The estate chosen for study in May 1979 lies in Selangor, on the west coast of Peninsular Malaysia; it belongs to one of the largest agency houses in the country. Parts of the estate have been bought up by foreign industrial companies and by the new local townships that are growing up along the Federal Highway.

However, large areas are still in production, substantial areas have undergone replanting and still other areas are converting to palm oil. This agency house is currently replanting in the south and central regions of Peninsular Malaysia, particularly in the states of Johore and Pahang. At the time of the fieldwork study, attempts were being made to relocate a section of the estate workforce, in family units, to these new areas.

The first task I set myself was the identification of the various forms of integration of the plantation household into capital accumulation within the wider plantation economy. My guiding hypothesis is that only by studying the processes of integration of the male, female and child estate labour into the accumulation of capital can we understand the household and family strategies of production and reproduction. It is only then that we can show precisely how the changes in wider plantation economy are affecting women and children.

The household's incorporation into the estate economy is dependent on two factors: the social division of labour, i.e., degree of task differentiation within the plantation, and the sexual division of labour within the household. The task differentiation within the plantation involves:

1. tapping the rubber tree: the cup is cleaned and turned up, scrap rubber is pulled

off from the previous day's cut and a strip is sliced off along the cut to start a fresh flow of latex;

2. latex collection: three to four hours after tapping, the latex in the cup is emptied into a bucket. The cup is put back facing the ground so that it will not fill with rain water. The bucket is carried to a collection centre to be sent to the factory for coagulation, pressing and smoking.

The daily work of field workers involves the care of the trees and land. Tasks include the weeding of undergrowth, the application of stimulants to the trees and the addition of fertilizers. In other words, the work on the rubber estates is labour-intensive and whole families can be put to work. The usual pattern until recently was one where the male head of the household was employed by the estate as the chief earner and was hence integrated into the plantation economy as a full-time wage worker. The woman of the household may be integrated as the second wage worker. Her participation as a full-time wage worker is dependent on the size and the age composition of the family. In large families where there are older daughters to look after the younger ones, the woman is often a full-time wage worker. Most of the women who are employed as full-timers work as field workers with pay much lower than tappers. In smaller families where the children are still young, the woman is employed as a temporary or casual worker, paid on a piece-rate basis. This picture is currently changing as the role of women undergoes restructuring.

For a long while women served as a manipulable labour force and as the reproducer of labour power and domestic life whose low wages through discriminatory wage scales enabled estates to expand.

In an economy where the level of technology required was minimal, in order to obtain the maximum in profit, the labour of women was used to lower the value of labour relative to capital. The women were almost always dependants of the male rubber tappers. These tappers were paid wages which were not adequate to cover their dependants' cost of living and reproduction. It was more profitable for the estates to employ the women at very low wages, often on a casual basis, together with the men rather than pay the latter higher wages. The women workers, being residents on the estate, also constituted a reserve tapping force used to fill in during absenteeism among the workers. Small plots are usually provided on the estates in the form of gardens. Women are responsible for these plots and grow some vegetables and fruit on them. Although insufficient to meet household requirements, the food on these plots does act as a supplement and allow low wages to be maintained on the estates.

The switch from rubber to palm oil has caused the displacement of over half the estate workforce. The labour force required on a palm oil estate is less than half that required on a rubber estate of an equal acreage. Workers retained by the plantations are retrained as harvesters on the palm oil estates. All harvesters are male workers. Women, usually dependants of the harvesters, are used as unskilled workers in maintenance and in collecting loose fruit from the ground during the harvest.

While part of the rubber land of the agency house under study was being converted into palm oil, other sections were being bought up by manufacturers and by real estate agents for conversion into industrial sites and new townships. This particular agency house was also replanting on cheaper tracts of land in Pahang and Johore, several hundred miles away, where there was a shortage of workers, especially experienced workers. Something was needed to keep a core of regular experienced workers accustomed to regular estate work and discipline. The offer made to the affected workers was to move them as *whole family units* to the new areas. This was not an attractive offer from the workers' point of view. Few liked the idea of uprooting themselves from an area where they had lived most of their lives. If part of the family remained behind, there were chances that their sons and daughters could find alternative employment in the new factories where they might be able to earn slightly higher wages. However, the idea of moving only part of the family unit was not what the estate authorities had in mind. The result was that workers who refused the offer to re-locate were served with notices to vacate their homes on the estate. If they did not do this they would lose all rights to their gratuity and be served with a court order.

The payment of the redundancy benefits shall be subject to the following special conditions:

(i) The maximum amount payable to any one person shall not exceed $600.

(ii) Payment shall fall due only when the retrenched worker and his dependants have left the estate and shall be made within one week of leaving. The worker shall forfeit his claim if he does not leave the estate within one month of the expiry of the period of his notice of such extended period as may be granted by the Manager in the circumstances of such case. Forfeiture of the claim does not deprive the Estate of any right it enjoys to take any appropriate action it may consider necessary to evict the worker from the Estate.

Provided that the payment shall not be forfeited if the retrenched worker elects to live with any of his children who may be employed on the estate and to whom a housing unit has been allocated. Provided further that he undertakes to vacate the housing unit and leave the estate should his continue occupancy of his children's housing unit infringe the regulations of the health or labour authorities.

(iii) Employees who have been declared redundant and for whom alternative employment is available in another estate of the same company in the same type of post or another post which will offer him approximately the same rate of emoluments shall not be eligible for any benefits under this agreement. If he rejects such alternative employment, he shall forfeit all claims or benefits under this agreement. If he accepts such alternative employment, his service with the previous estate shall be regarded as continuous.

(iv) Employees who have been declared redundant and to whom work has been offered in another estate belonging to a different company shall be entitled to the benefits under this agreement.

(v) Service which shall count for the purpose of the computation of the benefits under this agreement shall be permanent or checkroll service from the age of 14 years and upwards.[25]

In an area where there are employment alternatives, retrenchment does not necessarily lead to impoverishment, particularly for the young estate workers. However, for the old estate workers, retrenchment frequently means homelessness, unless one of their dependants continues to be employed by the Estate.

At the time of my fieldwork, a number of families were undergoing a crisis due to the re-location of new planting by the estate. In order not to forfeit their redundancy payments, many families were leaving the estates' premises. This action accelerated the squatter movement as families were forced out of the estate; they resorted to setting up illegal houses alongside railway tracks and nearby vacant lands where they could engage in some subsistence agriculture while their children searched for jobs in the industrial sector.

With the setting up of factories and the building of new towns there is also a tremendous demand for construction workers. A substantial number of displaced women workers find work, but only as casual, unskilled labourers for contractors and building firms. They are not paid a fixed wage but are used intermittently by the contractors whenever there are odd-jobs like brick-picking and sweeping to be done.

Problems of Estate Women and Children

In a situation where traditionally there is a demand for unskilled workers, the survival strategy of the estate workers is not to improve the 'quality' of their labour but to maximize the number of wage earners in the family; in other words, to have a large number of children. The average number of children until recently was seven per family. Some of the women interviewed also mentioned that it is only when they are pregnant that they get days off from work with pay. On this estate the women get eight weeks maternity leave with pay – M$90.00 (approx. £18) before confinement and the same amount after confinement. Before 1977, this applied to all the children that the women had. However, since 1977, this applied only to their first three pregnancies.

With the low wages and large family size, many households on the estate have great difficulty providing adequate food for their children. These households usually take food on credit from the estate grocery shops and borrow from money-lenders. The better-off households (households with at least two wage earners) borrow not to buy food but to buy consumer items like radios, bicycles, and sewing machines. Indebtedness is a common problem and it is common while visiting the estate to see creditors and money-lenders waiting at the house or office on payday. In situations where indebtedness has reached an advanced stage, it is the women who suffer most as they are the ones harassed by the money-lenders being the one usually at home. Whatever possessions the women have are sold or pawned to repay debts. They have to struggle for control over cash income. In these households, the problem of indebtedness is often compounded by the problem of alcoholism as it is common to find the husband spending a substantial proportion of his wages on toddy, an alcoholic drink commonly consumed in estates. In fact, the toddy shops have come to be termed by the women as 'the estate bank' as they are the place where the men visit on payday and leave behind their money.

Because of poverty, from an early age, about 6 – 7 years, children are used as unpaid workers by their parents, or are unofficially employed as part-time workers by the estate. As unpaid workers, they accompany their parents to the worksite by 6.00 a.m. Their main job is to remove the scrap rubber from the cups and the bark before the

3. *Day nursery on Prang Besar rubber plantation, Malaysia. (Photo: ILO).*

tapping. This speeds up the work of the parents and therefore increases their incentive payment. The ability to produce above the daily production quota through the use of unpaid child labour or the unpaid labour of stateless women is registered as higher labour production per man by the estate, overlooking that in reality, the surplus is produced by more than one person. When children are employed by the estate, their main job is to go around putting fertilizers at the foot of the rubber trees after school hours.

The crèche facilities leave much to be desired. Many crèches are based in old sheds with poor water and sanitation facilities. The crèche in the estate under study is better in this respect as it is located in a better building with proper water and sanitation facilities. However, there are hardly any toys or educational material and the children are more or less left to look after themselves under the supervision of two 'ayahs' or older estate women.

With the participation of women as full-time workers, the estate has actually encouraged smaller family size and has set up a family planning unit within the plantation. The small size of the family, however, does not change women's responsibility for reproduction of domestic life and labour power. This reproduction is both a short-run and long-run process; in the short-run, labour power, or the capacity for work, is produced and reconstituted on a daily basis through the production and consumption of use value. For the estate women living in a nuclear family, the most common household form, daily maintenance activities include the labour time expended on cooking, gathering fuel, hauling water, cleaning and washing clothes. Family members must also be nurtured and cared for, both on a daily basis and over time. These activities range from child-care to education. It is the woman who is faced with the day to day pressures of bringing up children, physically and psychologically.

According to the women interviewed, a full-time working woman is up by 4.00 a.m., collecting water for the day and preparing food for the worksite. There is usually one stand-pipe shared by six families and the water flow is controlled; there is water for only 2 – 3 hours a day. Electricity is also controlled. The lights come on at between 4.00 – 6.00 a.m. in the mornings and again in the evenings from 6.00 p.m. to 10.00 p.m. Children below the age of four years are sent to the crèche before 5.45 a.m. In many crèches there is no running water or facilities for boiling, and mothers bring along flasks of hot water and milk. Older children usually help out not only domestically, but also accompany their parents for roll-call at 5.45 a.m.

Tapping is usually completed by 10.00 a.m. However to allow for maximum drip, latex is not collected until 12.00 noon. The collection of latex from the cups, the queuing for the latex to be weighed, and the collection of latex by tankers for the rubber factory means that the woman is not home until 3.00 p.m. After 3.00 p.m. her domestic responsibility begins. The main tasks of the afternoon are the collection of fuel, particularly firewood as this is free, and the collection of water for washing clothes and cooking.

The women who become full-time estate employees are those who have access to child labour to help in the reproductive activities and on the worksites. In other words, women's position in the labour process is tied to the use of unpaid child labour as a means to increase the level of subsistence for the household and to generate a

4. *Women selecting germinated seeds on Prang Besar rubber estate, Malaysia. (Photo: ILO).*

TABLE 5.5   Composition of Full-Time Workers

Year	Male	Female
1974	132	209
1975	125	223
1976	118	228
1977	100	199
1978	85	146

SOURCE: Estate Reports.

surplus for the plantation. In particular, the women's participation as full-time workers is highly dependent on the availability of older daughters to act as substitutes for domestic work.

In the estate studied, all the women are employed in one way or another if they are Malaysian citizens. This is because, under the estate system, the single male wage earner would not be able to maintain a household even at subsistence level on his low wages. Table 5.5 shows the composition of the full-time permanent workers by sex composition for the estate:

Only women with red identity cards (non-citizens) are not employed. These are estate workers who failed to register themselves as citizens during the appropriate period or who are unable to produce their birth certificates. They are regarded as stateless and are the first to be retrenched. These women assist their husbands in latex collecting without additional payment, i.e., they are unpaid workers. Because of the scarcity of male labour on this estate, stateless males are employed under the work permit system.

I asked women who served under the discriminatory wage scales and are now serving under the equal wage scales, i.e. the old women tappers, to compare employment conditions under the two systems. The general consensus is that while women are better off economically today, their subordination has increased in other ways. For example, under the equal pay scales, women are expected to do ladder tapping (i.e. carry a four-foot ladder around to tap 300–400 trees, sometimes on hilly grounds) even when they are pregnant. One notable case was of a woman who had to ladder tap up to the eighth month of her pregnancy. Miscarriages are frequent.

The plantation authorities also insist on a clear separation between production and reproduction. Before the equal pay system was introduced, women were allowed to visit their children at the crèche or go about their household chores while waiting for the latex to drip. Now this behaviour could cause a woman tapper to be suspended from her work by the kangany. She is expected to be at the worksite, and to have allocated the reproductive activities to her older child.

The use of children, particularly daughters, from an early age as domestic substitutes and as unpaid or cheap labour on the worksites very often means the children are given the minimum of schooling. They attend the estate vernacular schools, drop out early, and replace their parents in estate work.[26] Schools are run by the estate, not really to educate estate children but more to keep them occupied. The struggle to

5. *Liquid rubber collected in pails by Chinese rubber tappers, Prang Besar, Malaysia. (Photo: ILO).*

maintain life at subsistence level means that manual work, the multiplicity of tasks, and the insecurity that comes from being positioned at one of the lowest ranks of the job hierarchy, drain whatever creative mental energy the children may have so that their educational development is limited. Together with this, the overcrowding in 'line-site houses' reinforces the social trap of poverty for the children and their parents. The heavily-guarded barrack-like houses within the estates were established to ensure control over the estate workforce and to separate them from the 'communist threat', which the authorities say still exists[27]. Security checks are put on visitors to the estates. These centralized settlements separate the estate workers from basic urban services and alternative income-generating activities, unless the estates are situated along the main trunk road, and are near the towns. What results is the creation of an insulated sub-system within the larger society. Recently, however, efforts are being made to improve the housing conditions for estate workers. In three estates, new housing schemes have been set up. These estates are Tennmaran Estate in Selangor, Carey Island Estate in Selangor, and one estate in the northern state of Kedah. In these schemes, water and electricity are more readily available and this has reduced the burden of women's domestic chores. The workers I interviewed say that it is difficult to gain access to these houses, since persons on whom the responsibility of allocation rests, often allocate the houses to themselves, their kin and their favourites.

Besides the higher risks of dropping out early from schools, daughters also suffer from the threat of rape. On the worksites, the girls are usually alone for long periods. The allocation of work tasks according to plots means that workers are frequently separated from each other by substantial distances. This, together with the thick undergrowth, makes it difficult for workers to be within sight of each other, particularly since work begins by 6.00 a.m. when it is still dark. Women employed as weeders face additional problems related to the use of the poisonous weed killer, paraquat. Many women due to constant exposure to this chemical suffer from impaired eye-sight, including blindness, bleeding nose, vomiting, lost of finger nails.

Conclusion

There has been an improvement in these women's status economically with the abolition of discriminatory wage scales and the recent creation of alternative employment which pays better wages has pressurized the estates to improve some conditions of life for the estate workforce as a whole. While the estate has not seen it sufficiently profitable to change the rhythm of rubber estate work, improvement has taken place in housing conditions for some estate workers. However, the switch from rubber to palm oil in sections of the estate has had differential impact on male and female labour, and in different groups of women workers. While some women are encouraged to shift into full-time estate work, many other women are displaced.

The inequality confronting women arising from the organization of the estate system, the norms and ideology operating among the estate workers and the heavy work burden of women have all contributed to women's subordination. Not only are there the intensification of their work tasks, the performance of new and often hazardous jobs (e.g., ladder-tapping, which was formerly done solely by men), but also the increasing use of daughters of school-going age as full-time domestic substitutes. Thus, the utilization of child labour is directly linked to the reorganization of the adult sexual division of labour.

The many difficulties faced by the woman in her productive and reproductive roles are seldom addressed by the trade union. Since there are now more women than men in the labour force of the estate, it is imperative that the needs and specific problems faced by women form an integral part of future planning of both the estates and the trade union with special attention shown to women casual workers. It is only recently that attempts have been made by some women trade unionists and some community development women workers to take up many of these issues and to encourage the discussion of these issues among the women themselves. Through this process, estate women are becoming more conscious of their own situation and are organizing and pressing for changes. This aspect will be discussed in Chapter 8.

Notes and References

1. Jackson, J., 1968, *Planters and Speculators*, University of Malaya Press, Kuala Lumpur.
2. Allen, G.C. and Donnithorne, A., 1957, *Western Enterprise in Indonesia and Malaya*, Macmillan, New York.
   Bauer, P.T., 1948, *The Rubber Industry*, Harvard University Press, Cambridge.
   Knorr, K.E., 1945, *World Rubber and Its Regulation*, Stanford University Press, Stanford.
3. Sandhu, Kernial Singh, 1969, *Indians in Malaya: Some Aspects of Their Immigration and Settlement* (1786–1957), Cambridge University Press, Cambridge.
   Mills, Lennox A., 1942, *British Rule in Eastern Asia*, Oxford University Press, London.
4. Sandhu, 1969, op. cit.
5. Straits Settlement Ordinance No. 5, 1984, quoted in Sandhu, 1969, op. cit.
6. Despatch No. 397 from Straits Settlements to Secretary of State, September 24, 1887, quoted in Sandhu, 1969, op. cit.
7. Agent of the Government of India Annual Report, 1928, quoted in Bauer, P.T., 1960, *Colonial Labour Policy and Administration*, London.
8. Planters' Association of Malaya Circular No. 12, 1931, quoted in Bauer, 1960, op. cit.
9. Ibid.
10. Federated Malay States, 1914, *Labour Department Annual Report*. Perak, 1914, *Labour Annual Report*.
11. McFadyean, 1945, (ed.) *The History of Rubber Regulation 1934–1943*, London.
12. Malacca Agricultural Medical Board, 1922, *Doctors' Annual Report*.
13. Planters' Association of Malaya, 1931, Circular No. 10, quoted in Bauer, 1960, op. cit.
14. Ibid.
15. An elastic substance, occurring naturally, as in natural rubber, or produced synthetically.
16. Edwards, Chris, 1977, 'Rubber in the World Economy,' *Pacific Research*, Vol. III, No. 6, September–October 1977, California.
17. Wasserman, Ursula, 1972, 'The Challenge of Synthetics', *Journal of World Trade Law*, Vol. 6, No. 3, May–June.
18. Conway, Sean, 1980, 'Natural Rubber Gaining Ground Ahead of New Agreements', *The Times*, London, 29 September 1980.
19. Courtenay, P.P., 1979, 'Some Trends in the Peninsular Malaysia Plantation Sector, 1963–1973', in J. Jackson and M. Rudner (eds), *Issues in Malaysian Development*,

Heinemann Educational Books, Kuala Lumpur.

20. *Far Eastern Economic Review*, 1978, Hong Kong, 15 September.

21. The MPIEA was dissolved in 1966 and re-organized as the Malayan Agricultural Producers' Association (MAPA).

22. National Union of Plantation Workers, 'Commitments for the Future', Plantation Workers' House, Selangor, Malaysia (no date).
National Union of Plantation Workers, 1967, 'Collective Bargaining in the Rubber Industry', Kuala Lumpur.

23. The Malaysian Government's definition of poverty line is based on the basic nutritional needs.

24. Peacock, Frank, 1979, 'The Failure of Rural Development in Peninsular Malaysia', in J. Jackson and M. Rudner (eds), *Issues in Malaysian Development*, Heinemann Educational Books, Kuala Lumpur.

25. Agreement of Redundancy Benefits between the Malayan Agricultural Producers' Association and the National Union of Plantation Workers.

26. Colletta, Nat, 1977, 'Class and Cultural Manifestations of Malay Education in a Plantation Context', in John Lent (ed.), *Cultural Pluralism in Malaysia: Polity, Military, Mass Media, Education, Religion and Social Class*, Centre for South-east Asian Studies, Northern Illinois University, Report No. 14.

27. *New Straits Times*, 1979, Kuala Lumpur, 25 September.

CHAPTER 6

Women and the Relocation of the Textile Industry

Industrialization and Relocation in South-East Asia

One of the major strategies of development in South-East Asia is export-led industrialization. With the take-off of export-oriented industrialization, young unmarried women or married women without children have been mobilized into the workforce on an unprecedented scale. The question that needs investigation is why is there an overwhelming presence of young women in certain industries? The mobilization trend constitutes a break with the past and on the face of it opens new channels for emancipation for young women, the bulk of whom are migrants from the rural areas. However, new forms of subordination have also emerged. There has been a restructuring in the lifestyles of these young women as new norms of behaviour and culture are introduced to the workers; they are subjected to a variety of work-related health and social problems for which their employers are in no way held responsible, they are subjected to inevitable male supervisory strata to which they have limited mobility and often they are paid wages which force them to reduce their individual expenditures by living in over-crowded conditions and reducing the quality of their food intake.

This chapter addresses itself to these trends. It focuses on two questions regarding the nature of industrial employment for young women. First, why are young women concentrated in certain labour-intensive industries in South-East Asia? Secondly, to what extent and in what way is this employment emancipatory for the women who are employed? These questions are examined within the context of the textile industry, an industry which employs the largest number of young women in Asia and within the context of the relationship of these industries within South-East Asian societies.

The Export Processing Zones (EPZs)

Governments in the region have been very successful in attracting large investments from international companies by the use of special policies such as the creation of 'export processing zones' (EPZs) or 'free trade zones' (FTZs), containing 'world market factories' producing mainly for export. These new policies have given a significant new push to industrial growth and employment in many of these countries, as they ensure low wages, tax incentives, the provision of industrial and business infrastructure and the control over labour.[1]

An EPZ is a relatively small, geographically separated area within a country, created for the sole purpose of attracting export-oriented industries by offering them favourable investment and trade conditions as compared with the remainder of the host country. It is an area created to provide for the duty-free re-entry of goods assembled abroad from parts and components exported from the developed countries. Besides being exempted from normal import and export regulations, EPZs are also exempted from other kinds of regulations such as protective labour legislation, taxation law, and laws about transfer of profits.

Most states in South-East Asia also impose tight control over their workforce through control on unionization, restrictive legislation, and the use of state machinery that is through deregistration, detention and the recognition of only state or factory control unions.

The attractive 'package deals' offered to those who set up world market factories in export processing zones have attracted considerable investment. They represent a movement of production from the developed countries to South-East Asia.[2] The most important industries are textiles, clothing and electronics. For example, nineteen EPZs in South-East Asia have textile factories, eighteen have clothing factories, and fourteen have electronic companies as seen in Table 6.1. Other goods being produced are shoes, toys, sporting equipment, travel goods, watches, radios and TVs, furniture, wigs and car spares.

At first sight this looks like a motley collection of 'old' and 'new' industries; 'traditional' products like textiles and clothing, toys and furniture; more sophisticated metal products like car spares; and the modern 'new technology' electrical and electronic industries. But the modern industries have not completely relocated to Third World factories. The most highly knowledge-intensive processes of electronics design have remained in the US and Japan. The relocated parts of the electronics industries are assembly and test operations which are standardized, repetitious and requiring much labour. Most industries that have moved to the new world market factories are difficult or costly to automate further and are highly labour-intensive.

TABLE 6.1   Manufacturing activities in EPZs, 1975

Textiles	19
Clothing	18
Electronics	14
Metals products	11
Precision instruments	11
Leather and shoes	10
Machinery	9

SOURCE: Adapted from Frobel, *et al.*, The New International Division of Labour, Hamburg, 1977.

In the textile industry, considerable relocation has occurred to some Third World countries. In the 1970s, over one million jobs in the textile industry disappeared in Western Europe.[3] West Germany alone lost 102,000 textile jobs, while in France there was a wave of textile plant closures and bankruptcies, causing a loss of 25,000 jobs.[4] During this period, employment in the Hong Kong textile industry increased four times. In South Korea and Taiwan, one out of every three new jobs created in the 1960s was in textiles.[5] It has been estimated that thirty per cent of trousers and sixty per cent of shirts sold in Europe in the late 1970s were made by Asian women.[6]

The major factors which make relocation easier are the following:

1. *Technological changes in transport and communication.* The development of air freight and ship containerization has lowered transport costs among all those locations which are close to ports and airports. Relocation is also made easier by developments in telecommunications systems and data processing techniques.

2. *Wages.* Wage rates and associated social costs have been rising faster in advanced countries than in many Third World countries. The *Far Eastern Economic Review* (18 May 1979, p. 18) reported that

> Wages for unskilled and semi-skilled labour in Asian Free Trade Zones are between a tenth and one-eighth of those in the West, and total working times per year, because of overtime hours, fewer holidays and longer working hours are up to fifty per cent higher than in Western factories. Social overhead costs, in the form of social security payments, fringe benefits, travel, uniform, and other allowances are only twenty to thirty per cent of the total payment compared with eighty per cent in the West.[7]

However, when compared to many local companies, large-scale foreign companies still provide better wages.

3. *Technological changes in the production process.* Relocation can be made easier by technical changes in the production process. For example, the overall production process can be split up into small tasks which can be learned rapidly and used routinely. In engineering and particularly electronics, it has been possible to break down the production process and to transfer abroad those parts which are labour-intensive.

From the position of the South-East Asian States, part of the logic of the export-led industrialization is the 'employment crisis'. As discussed in Chapter 2, poverty has been intensified for the lowest strata of rural society. In many areas, government and international programmes for rural development have resulted in concentrating resources, land, technology, training, etc. in the hands of the middle-level and large-scale farmers. There is growing landlessness which is aggravated by the pressure of population. The restructuring in the plantation sector, as discussed in Chapter 5 has resulted in a relocation and displacement of entire families.

Many rural income-generating activities have failed to provide real security with households existing at a precarious level (see Chapter 3). These activities are further threatened through contact with the urban and industrial areas. The intrusion of

6. *Work in a plant producing toilet articles and detergent, Thailand. Ninety-five per cent of the workforce are women. (Photo: ILO).*

urban interests into the rural areas has resulted in many handicrafts producers and traders being almost completely displaced by competition from factory manufactured goods. With little security in the rural areas, pressures are set up for migration to urban areas in search of employment. Besides an escape from rural poverty, urban employment is also seen as a means of escape from the restrictions and hardship of rural life and as exposure to new opportunities.

While these factors help to set the attraction of labour-intensive industries within a broad prospective, they do not explain why, even with the presence of male unemployment, young women make up more than 70 per cent of specific labour-intensive industries such as textiles, electronics, food processing, and toy manufacturing in Indonesia, Thailand, Malaysia, the Philippines and Singapore. In other words, why is there an overwhelming presence of young women in certain industries?

This chapter focuses on young women in the textile industry. This is, firstly, on account of the overall importance of the industry. After food production, it is the biggest industrial sector, and it is more compact to study than the diverse food industry. Although more compact, the textile industry has wide differences in size of company, level of technology, and multinational control. Textile and clothing sales account for about one-fifth of global retail sales, reflecting the fact that textile goods are so basic that almost all the world's population buys them.

The second reason to study the textile industry is that it is a large employer. It has been estimated that 107 million people earn wages from the textile industry, quite apart from farmers who produce cotton, and clothes makers who work from home.[8] It is a relatively labour-intensive industry even after rationalization and technological changes in the advanced countries.

Thirdly and finally, the textile industry is one which has relocated and employs mainly young women workers. The reason for employing young women as the bulk of the workforce can only be understood if we examine first the crises in the textile industry. The next section gives some basic information on the textile industry, some reasons why relocation has taken place, and what the implications of relocation are for women workers in the industry.

The Structure of the Textile Industry

1. *Chemical fibre production.* Since the Second World War natural cotton fibres have come under competition from synthetic fibres, particularly polyester, nylon and acrylic. These are oil-based products mostly manufactured by large capital-intensive petrochemical companies in huge chemical plants. Big companies include Du Pont, Courtaulds, ICI and Hoechst. Only a few Third World countries have an internal market large enough to install such a plant.

By 1978, a few Third World countries had plants (Korea, Mexico and Brazil were the most important) producing seventeen per cent of the world's total production. However, members of OPEC are investing in such petrochemical industries. The industries are expensive investments but the oil feedstock is cheap and it is likely that the 1980s will see global overcapacity of synthetic fibres with relocation of production towards the oil-rich countries of the Third World.

The increasing use of synthetics has allowed the acceleration of textile production. Synthetic fibres are stronger, do not break so easily, and are smoother and do not get caught at high input speeds, so weaving and knitting looms have been automated to a higher degree for synthetics than for cotton textiles.

2. *Textile cloth production* was one of the earliest industries to be established in Asian countries. India's textile industry, broken in the early colonial period, expanded rapidly in the early part of this century with major investments in factories. Textile cloth production is technologically one of the easier industries to set up from scratch. There is a large number of machinery manufacturers, and large quantities of second-hand machinery. The various processes are well-known, not patented, and not tightly integrated. At least that was the case until the 1970s. Until then, technical changes had been small for almost a century. Since then increased automation of spinning and the introduction of shuttleless weaving looms have slowly been introduced increasing productivity by two and a half to six times. Even so, relocation continued to take place until tariff barriers were erected against the Third World producers in many EEC countries.

The textile industry is a major employer of industrial labour in Asia. Korea, for example, has 700,000 workers in these industries. The two largest Korean textile companies are among the World's top twenty-five textile companies. The mainspring of Hong Kong's industrialization in the 1950s was the textile industry. Data from the late 1960s showed that the Hong Kong textile looms and factories were operating twenty-four hours a day, 365 days a year. The textile industry had some of the worst working conditions in the colony. No other country came within twenty-five per cent of this level of machinery use. The wages in Hong Kong were one-eighth of those in the US, and the productivity was one-fourth, illustrating the competitiveness of Hong Kong in relation to the US.[9]

3. *Garment making.* This is the most labour-intensive part of the process. Here cloth is cut and then sewn into garments. This is where the Third World countries have transformed the market. Their share of the market has increased from nineteen to thirty-seven per cent between 1965 and 1977. It has been said that except for petroleum, the garment flow from developing to developed countries is unmatched by any other commodity. Significant trade surpluses are found in the clothing industries of the Newly Industrializing Countries (NICs), consisting of Hong Kong, South Korea and Taiwan.

Many have tried to lobby against import restrictions. They include the small companies who have been increasingly squeezed and liquidated and have joined with those campaigning for restrictions on imports of cloth and garments from the Asian NICs and other Third world countries. The Multi Fibre Agreement, began in 1973, set a quota system on such imports from East Asia (Korea, Taiwan and Hong Kong). Some textile companies in these three countries reacted by setting up companies in South-East Asia in Singapore, the Philippines, and Indonesia. In South-East Asia, the vast majority of garment factories are owned by investors from East Asia and South Asia (in Thailand) rather than by multinationals.

The reasons for the use of young women workers have been associated with the current pressures of competition in the international market which has forced firms to increase labour productivity while minimizing production costs. The reasons for using young women are usually given as the lower cost of female labour in comparison with the same category of male labour; the higher productivity of young women as opposed to men in some labour-intensive industries, including textiles; and the social and cultural attitudes of young women which allow a high degree of social control and predictability. Young Asian women are known for their respect for authority.

The three reasons given above for the widespread use of women's labour will be made clear by looking at the employment conditions in the South-East Asian textile industry, and comparing them with the shipbuilding industry which employs mainly men.

Women's Work – Employment and Recruitment in the Textile Industry

If women form a source of cheap, productive and pliable labour, why are they not found in more industrial sectors as they would be attractive in any profit-making enterprise? This section looks at recruitment and work conditions in two parts of the textile industry; textile cloth production and garment manufacture. Although the work processes are different, and require different kinds of workers, both parts of the industry mostly recruit women.

However, as we shall see, recruitment strategies make use of differences other than gender. Age, educational levels, ethnic origins, and rural–urban differences are all used in mobilizing different kinds of workforce for the textile industry. There are two general reasons for this, wages and skills; and a wide range of more specific reasons. First the general reasons.

Both cloth and garment manufacturers commonly recruit young women workers for the factories and older women with children (i.e. housewives) as outworkers for the garment industry. Female labour is almost always cheaper than the same category of male labour. As women, they are classified in the labour market as 'secondary workers', and, unlike male workers, are paid wages that do not cater for the reproduction of the family. In other words, women are usually paid subsistence but not a family wage. In the textile industry in Hong Kong, women's wages in the factories, for example, were about thirty per cent lower than those of men. Asian women, are also said to have 'keener eyesight' and 'naturally nimble fingers' for speed and accuracy in production and docility in behaviour that makes them more suitable than men for work that is monotonous and repetitious.[10]

There are specific reasons to recruit women for the different processes. Cloth manufacture is essentially a machine-tending industry. Work techniques are incorporated into the machine, and the technology and division of labour reduce the workers' (mainly female workers') control over their work process to a minimum.

In the cloth manufacturing industry, labour that is diligent but cheap and easy to control is needed for the production lines. Young women, with some years of schooling, from small towns and rural areas are usually mobilized by the urban-based factories. In Peninsular Malaysia, the majority of Malay women working in the Free

7. *Spinning mill, Republic of Korea. (Photo: ILO).*

Trade Zones are rural migrants. In the Subang-Sungei Way Free Trade Zone on the West Coast of Peninsular Malaysia, young rural Malay women are estimated to make up seventy per cent of the total female workforce in 1979. My study of the textile industry in the Jurong industrial estate of Singapore in 1975 – the largest industrial site in the country – found that unlike in the electronics industry, the majority of young girls working in cloth manufacturing are Malaysian migrants, largely Chinese, from the rural areas or small towns. These girls are new to industrial work, coming from a background of small family business or subsistence farming where the rhythm of work is organized around the household.

A substantial proportion of the young women workers are fresh school leavers in their first job. Where some have been employed previously, this former employment is very likely to be in 'informal sector' jobs like domestic service and seamstressing, particularly in piece work for garment industries. For example, two-thirds of the women workers in the Bayan Lepas FTZ in Malaysia in 1973 were new entrants to the wage labour market; in 1975, less than twenty per cent of the workers in the same zone had been previously employed, mostly in farming, domestic service, seamstressing and sales.

In the Singapore textile factor where I took a job as a textile worker, eighty per cent of the female workforce were migrants from Malaysia and twenty per cent were Singaporeans. Given the presence of alternative employment in air-conditioned, cleaner electronic factories, local women prefer not to work in the textile industry where the work environment is harsh and the noise and dust levels high. The Singaporean women who are employed in the factory normally occupy a much higher job position than the migrants, independent of educational level and years of service. As citizens, they have better chances of promotion than the migrants, and are often made overseers or assistant overseers. While the Singaporean workers seek job promotion by staying at a particular workplace, the migrant workers tend to seek promotion by 'job-hopping'. After accumulating a certain amount of industrial experience, they see their chances of mobility as higher across industries than within a particular factory, especially in a situation where new industries are being set up and are on the look out for workers with some industrial background. This trend is now changing as the government has brought in legislation to prevent work permit holders, largely Malaysians, from changing their jobs for at least three years. This legislation was introduced in response to pressures created by employees to prevent newly established firms from 'stealing' workers who have adjusted successfully to the rhythm of the textile industry.

Recruitment of young girls from Malaysian villages into Singapore-based factories takes place through the use of agents. These agents usually approach clan organizations and local political party branches for help. In Indonesia, male agents recruit village girls for the textile industry through the help of local male dignitaries.[11] These people are usually religious leaders or school teachers, and have more influence over the daily lives of the villagers than government bureaucracy. By recruiting in this way, a substantial part of the labour force has been selected, based on their understanding of the traditional obligations which require gratitude to those who have helped them gain employment. This sense of gratitude ensures a certain amount of compliance as any trouble from the employees would also mean a 'loss of face' for the people who recommended them.

Given their socialization within Muslim and traditional Chinese patriarchal societies, women, particularly young women, are used to their subordinate position in the male-dominated households and villages from which they come. These girls are employed because they are 'easy to control', 'pleasant' 'nice', 'co-operative', 'do not answer back'. In fact one firm in Peninsular Malaysia which employed 300 males out of its 4,000 production operators experienced great 'discipline problems' with the male operators refusing to obey certain instructions from supervisors. These male workers were also described by the employers as being 'too impatient and ambitious' as compared to the young women workers. The young girls are also said to have 'keener eyes and agile hands' to spot and repair breakage in the yarn.

All the young women workers in the cloth manufacturing industry have had some years of schooling. The number of years in school vary, being highest among the Malaysian migrants in Singapore (more than half of whom have some secondary schooling) and lowest among rural migrants from the hinterlands of Jakarta, Indonesia where most of the rural recruits have spent only a few years in school. These firms use formal schooling as a recruitment strategy as schooling usually differentiates people who have 'stuck it out' in the system which encourages con-scientiousness and discipline from those who have not. Employers think that workers who have had at least some years of schooling are better able to bear the long hours of meticulous, tedious and monotonous work than workers who have had no schooling.

As electronic industries also compete for young women workers in the same country some differentiations have been created among the young women workers themselves. The electronics industry has higher educational requirements than the textile industries in all the South-East Asian countries examined. While the textile industry recruits young women with some primary schooling, the electronic indus-tries demand at least some secondary schooling. Increasingly electronics workers are expected to have completed their secondary education, that is, they are expected to have eight years of schooling.

Foreign firms also require higher educational qualifications from their workers than do indigenous firms. In the Republic of Singapore, for example, foreign elec-tronics firms have raised the educational standards required of a female factory worker before she is given wage employment. Educational level and gender are also used to differentiate supervisors from production workers. Almost all the production workers in the cloth manufacturing industry are young women workers. Males with some secondary education are recruited as machinists, machine maintenance operators and apprentices to technicians. For the purposes of supervision, males from the urban areas with advanced-level secondary education or from institutions of higher education like the polytechnics are recruited. There are few female super-visors. Management fairly commonly believe that these males are better at social control; they know how to keep their distance and are better at giving orders from the management and seeing that these instructions are carried out. Also, in the Republic of Singapore, these males have had some years of military training.

Compared to textile manufacturing, industrial garment manufacture involves one woman to one sewing machine; the work is done in a relatively dustless environment and involves the use of skills in which the women workers are already trained. The techniques required are similar to that of the domestic sewing machine. Also unlike cloth manufacture, the garment industry lends itself to the put-out system of sub-contracting where women workers sew garments for the factories within the premises of their homes and are paid by the piece rate method.

The growth of the garment industry in Singapore, Thailand and the Philippines drew workers from traditional crafts. In Singapore, these workers were women involved in household-based tailor shops producing cheap garments for the local clientele in neighbourhoods surrounding the shops. Some of these shops also provided sewing lessons for the girls in the neighbourhood during the evenings. With the growth of the garment industry producing for the mass market locally the abroad, these small household-based shops underwent a variety of changes. Some of them continued their production but began changing their clientele. Besides catering for the neighbourhood customers, many of these shops began sewing for the more fashionable boutiques that were sprouting up in the numerous shopping centres and hotels in Singapore. These boutiques cater to a sophisticated clientele who wanted clothing different from that produced by the factories for the mass market.

Several of the tailor shops, the ones which could not convert their cutting and designing skills to suit the sophisticated market, went out of business as their market declined since many local girls bought ready made garments produced by the factories. The girls working in the tailor shops found it more secure working for the factories receiving a guaranteed wage at the end of each month.

In the factory itself, the labour force consists mainly of young women workers, the majority of whom have had some experience with sewing machines. But there are also girls who have no work experience but had to do sewing as part of their household chores. Besides employing young women, many garment factories use home workers. These home workers may be rural or urban housewives i.e. older women with children to care for at home. In the Bataan EPZ in Philippines in 1978 for example, there was an estimate of a thousand garment factories employing about 500,000 workers who were housewives in rural-based cottage industries.[12] In Singapore, many of the small urban tailorshops receive contracts from the garment industry and local housewives (frequently friends or kin of the factory girls) are employed as homeworkers, on a piece-rate basis, whenever the factories receive large overseas orders.

The sub-contracting arrangement provides the garment industry with a workforce that is at its disposal only when there is a demand for their labour. At other times, this labour force is not its responsibility. Also, the homeworkers provide the industry with a very cheap source of labour as they are paid on a piece-rate basis and the workers provide their own machines, electricity and work premises. One problem with the out-work arrangement is quality control. Because of this, most of the out-workers are women who are very skilled at machine-sewing and require no supervision, once instructions are given by agents from the factory.

Within the garment factory, there is a clear preference for using young female labour in parts of the production process that are classified as semi-skilled or unskilled. An examination of the sexual division of labour in the garment industry shows that hardly any women's work within this industry is treated as highly skilled work. In the Bataan Export Processing Zone in the Philippines, there are an estimated 1,000 garment factories employing 200,000 workers in 1978. Ninety-five per cent of the garment factory workers are young women in their early twenties.

They were employed for sewing. The higher-paid jobs of skilled cutters and pressers were filled by Filipino men. The latter job, although not skilled, is physically taxing and is regarded as a man's job.

The young women are classified as semi-skilled or unskilled because of the little time required for their 'on-the-job' training. In the garment industry, it is possible to master the basic skills of the job in about six weeks. This short training period, however, overlooks an important aspect of women's labour. The famous 'nimble fingers' of the young Asian girl are not a natural attribute but a skill acquired within the household from an early age for tasks defined sexually as 'women's role'. These skills are easily transferred to certain factory operations and because the training is 'socially invisible' having taken place within the origins of the domestic sphere, the skills are treated as innate or biologically determined. Jobs that make use of these skills are classified as unskilled and semi-skilled.

To make a comparison between predominantly women's work and predominantly men's work, we will now look at a description of a shipbuilding industry.

The Shipbuilding and Repairing Industry

The shipbuilding and repairing industry in Singapore is a traditional craft which has grown almost overnight into the fastest growing major industry. The juxtapositioning of these two industries will allow some comparisons to be made between the recruitment of an essentially male labour force with that of the young female workforce.

Unlike the cloth manufacturing industry, the growth of the shipbuilding industry required a substantial increase in skilled workers. The industries that supplied the skilled labour to the shipbuilding and repairing industry are largely the older traditional shipyards, contract labour, engineering firms and electrical shops, i.e. industries that are related to shipbuilding and repairing. Because of the rapid growth of the industry it was not possible to limit recruitment only to skilled workers from the traditional crafts. There were large investments by the government and the larger shipbuilding firms in training programmes. In the government-owned shipyards, adult training schemes were introduced to upgrade the skills of semi-skilled and unskilled workers who had been with the yard for about six years. I was told by the officials of these schemes that it was very easy to train these people as they already have acquired some of the basic skills and knowledge of work during their long years in the yard.

The off-the-job training usually lasts for six months. These organized training schemes are also a means of bonding the workers to the yard. In the initial period of rapid industrialization, one of the major problems is the shortage of skilled labour. In fact, the labour turnover in the shipyards was one of the highest among the industries because the newly established yards took away many of the skilled workers from the older yards by offering high wages.

Most foreign-owned yards have organized mass recruitment and training programmes to meet the need for developing a pool of skilled workers. In the early 1970s the largest foreign shipyard was recruiting two hundred migrant workers every three months for a period of three years. These recruits were sent to the local voca-

tional institutions for full-time training in the basic skills of shipbuilding. This training usually lasts for three months. Some of the two hundred new recruits are sent by
the firm to Japan for twelve months. These boys are bonded for five years and if they
break the bond, they are forced to repay the firm the total training cost. The officials
of this firm told me that they prefer migrant workers to Singaporeans because
migrants are forced by their work permit to stay with the firm for at least three years.

My interviews with the managers of the foreign shipyards about their recruitment
strategies indicate that foreign workers are recruited in groups from similar areas in
Malaysia. This means that the workplace is not a collection of individuals but of different groups of workers, as there are already established friendship patterns prior to
recruitment. The considerable degree of primary relationships among members of a
group is regarded by the firm as useful in helping the workers to adapt and stay on in
an industrial system of work in a foreign country.

Although male recruiting agents are sent by the yards to Malaysia initially, subsequent recruitment often takes place through the workers recommending their relatives and friends. The importance given to primary relationships in recruitment
brings about a pattern of social control based on reciprocal obligation. This method of
social control is fairly similar to that found among the young women workers.

What is different between shipbuilding and textile work, however, is firstly, the
absence of gender relationships as a system of social control in the shipyards;
secondly, emphasis is given to the stabilization of employment in the yards so that
these jobs may become careers. Such emphasis is missing for the young women
workers. Thirdly there is large investment in training programmes for the male workforce and an absence of such systematic training for the female workforce. These
differences are all the more pertinent if we compare the difference along gender lines
in what are regarded as skills. The male workers trained in traditional crafts are classified by the industrial shipyards as 'skilled workers' whereas the young women trained
professionally in garment production by the traditional household shops are regarded
as 'semi-skilled' or even 'unskilled'. Although the background in job training is
similar, i.e. both types of workers were trained by small-scale traditional workshops,
the category 'skilled work' is socially defined by the sex of the person.

To What Extent Emancipation?

Perhaps the single most important reason why individual women seek employment
in export-oriented factories is the belief that factory work offers an opportunity for
income, greater independence and a better future, if not for themselves at least for
their parental households. This section explores the extent to which emancipation
takes place through factory work. What are some of the new possibilities that earning
a wage generates? What are some new problems created by such work?

1. *Income and expenditure.* Wages earned by women workers in labour intensive
export industries are usually lower than those of equivalent male workers and below
the minimum subsistence level. The girls accept these wages out of necessity. In

urban areas like Singapore and Hong Kong, most working-class families require more than one wage earner to maintain a minimum or a slightly more comfortable standard of living. In predominantly Chinese countries older daughters tend to be sent out to work to provide for the education of younger siblings, especially sons.[13] In the predominantly Muslim societies of Malaysia and Indonesia, it is a customary obligation under Islamic law for parents to care for their daughters until marriage. In practice, young girls are pressured into marriage out of absolute economic necessity. Many Muslim girls now migrate to the urban factories as an alternative to these marriages, and are willing to accept subsistence wages. They reduce their individual expenditures by living together, often in over-crowded conditions in dormitories or rented rooms, and by reducing the quality of their food intake. Often they also get subsidies in the form of goods from relatives in the rural areas.

In fact, data from all five countries examined suggest that the girls in the textile factories earn low wages compared to other industrial sectors. The textile factories in the hinterland of Jakarta seem to pay the lowest wages among the five countries. In fact, 'the low wages they pay make it almost impossible for anyone with dependants to accept them'.[14] Even in conditions of high labour surplus, men in Muslim societies keep away from such work as under Islamic law, the authority vested in the male is also bound up with his ability to support his household. A man's failure to provide for his wife is one of the new reasons a woman is allowed divorce.[15]

In Singapore, where the wages for factory workers are regarded as one of the highest in South-East Asia, 68.5 per cent of all factory girls as compared to 23.6 per cent of males earned below $400 (Singapore) in 1982 i.e. approximately US$190 a month, as shown in Table 6.2. This figure is commonly regarded as a subsistence wage for a two-member household living in subsidized housing. So low are the wages of the textile workers that workers are able to save some of their income only when provided with free housing and subsidized food by the factories. Recently, this is done by 'bringing the workplace to the workers' i.e. by situating the factories near high-rise estates where workers live so that the girls can continue to live with their parents and at the same time contribute to the 'pooling of incomes' within the household.

TABLE 6.2 Workers Earning Under $400* a Month in 1982

Characteristics	Total	Number Under $400	Percentage
In All Industry (AI)	1,113,979	387,259	34.8
In Manufacturing Industries (MI)	334,021	143,599	43 0
Male Workers in AI	725,624	189,367	26.1
Male Workers in MI	189,773	44,733	23.6
Female Workers in AI	388,355	197,892	50.9
Female Workers in MI	144,248	98,864	68.5

SOURCE: Report on the Labour Force Survey of Singapore, 1982.

* In Singapore, this figure may be taken as subsistence wage for a two-member household in 1982, i.e. two adults living in a subsidized one-room flat and working in a factory within walking distance from their home.

As in Singapore, expenditure patterns in other East and South-East Asian countries, vary according to whether the worker lives at home with her family, or in a dormitory or rented accommodation near her place of work.[16] Workers who live at home contribute more of their income to their families. The amount that the girls actually contribute to their parental home varies according to the extent to which the girls are controlled by the traditional Chinese ideology of 'the good daughter'. This ideology defines a 'good daughter' as one who spends little on herself and gives most of what she has to her parents and younger siblings. A large number of rural migrants in Singapore conform to this ideology, saving and sending home as much as one-fifth of their small income.

In Hong Kong, a 1970 survey of 660 young factory workers aged between fourteen and twenty-one showed that forty per cent gave all of their income to their families. In Malaysia most of the young women workers give between twenty-five per cent and sixty per cent of their income to their families. The rest of the girls' wages are spent on their own basic needs.

2. *Conditions of employment.* Variations in conditions of employment occur according to countries and within countries according to size and ownership of the enterprises. Within each factory, variations also occur according to different kinds of jobs. Some of these variations are given in Table 6.3. In many of the countries, workers work very long hours, often working seven days a week. Safety and health conditions in the factories are poor, especially in the factories studied by researchers in the hinterland of Jakarta and in Hong Kong. In the Republic of Korea, the large-scale factories provide better working conditions, particularly in terms of fringe benefits compared to the small-scale factories.[17] The same may be said of Singapore. The largest textile factory I studied provided free housing and subsidized food for the workforce. However the working conditions within the factory itself remain poor. Cotton dust flies all over the roving sections, the girls in the packing section suffer skin irritations from the glues and chemicals used, the weaving section is extremely noisy and the Ministry of Labour has estimated that one in seven textile workers suffer from hearing trouble.

While it is not possible to rank the five countries according to the quality of technology used in their industries, there is evidence that many of the textile factories in the hinterland of Jakarta use low-level technology, often second-hand machinery from Taiwan. Most of these factories are ill-equipped and pay some of the lowest wages in South-East Asia. In contrast, the textile factories in Singapore and Seoul appear to be of a high technological standard. The machinery for spinning and weaving is modern and incorporates most of the manufacturing process. These factories provide better wages but there is little change in the work process itself. Workers are still needed essentially to mind the machines and to repair breakages in the yarn when these occur.

Besides technology, another factor that governs the conditions of employment is the ideology that determines how work should be organized. Most of the textile factories in the five countries seem to operate on the principle that greater production

TABLE 6.3 Work Conditions for Female Workers in the Textile Industry

Country	Average No. of Hours	Poor Health and Safety Conditions	Other Features	Evaluation by Researchers
Hong Kong	about half workers on full 7 days	Yes	N.A.	worst in E Asia
Republic of Korea (Seoul and hinterlands)	most female workers work $6\frac{1}{2}$ days	Yes	Physical abuse by managers; 3 shifts	high variation between small and large-scale industry
Singapore	about a fifth of workers work full 7 days	Yes (in cloth manufacture)	3 shifts	high variation according to firm. Hong Kong owned textile firms have the worst reputation
Philippines (Manila and hinterlands)	long working hours	Yes but improving in larger factories	N.A.	high variation according to ownership
Indonesia (Jakarta and hinterlands)	long working hours	Yes	very low pay 'gruelling shift work'	'appalling conditions'

and expanding profits are created by intensifying the work process and by strong social controls.

Intensification of the work process takes place firstly through the speeding up of production. In the Singapore textile factory, this is done by installing new faster machines for weaving, spinning and roving, as compared to those originally installed when the factory started its operation. Secondly by methods that are believed to increase the output of the workers. This is done through the use of economic incentives. In the largest Singapore textile factory workers are put on a task system followed by piece-rate. Using this system, in the roving section where raw cotton fibres are prepared for spinning, workers are organized into work groups. If the work groups are able to produce above a certain level, the workers are all given a bonus; however, if production levels are below the given figure, the workers are paid the basic wage for the day. A somewhat similar arrangement is worked out for the girls in the weaving section, although they work individually. Each weaver is in charge of six machines and if the total output for the day is above the given amount, the worker is given a bonus. Besides the piece-rate system, if workers are not absent for a whole month, they are given a small bonus of two days' pay and if they are willing to stop their annual leave they are again given a bonus of a month's pay.

Strong social controls are not only created through the use of the various hierarchies – gender, educational levels, rural/urban origins – discussed earlier, but also through the control of labour unions when these exist at all, and through the use of state machinery to check grassroot militancy. Available data shows that in 1977, ten per cent of the total workforce in Hong Kong was unionized; in the Republic of Korea, thirty per cent of the final factory workforce was organized and in Singapore fifty per cent of the female factory workers belonged to unions. The percentage of unionized workers however is no indication of the power or otherwise of the labour movement in these countries. In Hong Kong, it appears that trade unions do not generally defend or develop the rights of workers:[18] in the Republic of Korea, all strikes are forbidden under the Emergency (security) Decree; in Singapore all trade unions regarded by the authorities as 'left-wing' have been de-registered and the unions that are allowed to operate within the country have been co-opted as 'junior partners in development', keeping a strict check on wage claims and on strike actions. The high percentage of unionized workers in Singapore is mainly the result of the checklist system of recruitment in most of the large industrial enterprises. All workers are automatically made union members when they are recruited and their union fees are automatically deducted from their monthly salary. When grass-root militancy has occurred, the police were called in and the workers' leaders were sacked.

Employment in many of the export oriented industries has also been proved to be insecure. During the 1974 to 1975 world recession, three quarters of the 20,000 workers who lost their jobs in Singapore were women employed in the textile and electronics industry. In the Philippines, one survey showed that half of the workers interviewed had been laid off in 1975 for periods ranging from two weeks to nine months. For the worker who is laid off, re-hiring is by no means certain. However, younger workers are preferred as they are cheaper.[19] Often when re-hired, the experienced workers are paid only the starting wage. Lay-offs may be a response to global cyclical market fluctuations, but in many countries, companies may reduce their labour force or even close down because they are shifting to new cheaper locations – that is, re-relocation! Currently, as wages are rising and as Singapore is pushing for high skilled industries, many of the labour-intensive industries are relocating some of their production processes to cheaper South-East Asian countries like Malaysia, Indonesia and Thailand. In Singapore, local business interests have also developed using the models presented by the MNCs and have begun investing in cheaper neighbouring countries, including China.

3. *Forms of social and cultural behaviour*. Within the factory, young women workers are exposed to a number of social and cultural influences, some of which resemble the traditional culture of the background from which the girls had come, and some of which are quite different and require some adjustment.

The traditional patriarchial systems are not challenged within the factory. As already seen, although women form the bulk of the workforce, they are concentrated in the lower ranks of the industrial hierarchy. The supervisory grades are occupied mainly by men. In fact, values of traditional society which make for workers' productivity are encouraged. These values include obedience to authority, hard work, honesty, discipline and self-denial.

Whei e workers have come from predominantly rural backgrounds, their values are likely ιo be those of a co-operative life with emphasis put on the family and community rather than on the individual worker. Many factories in Malaysia and Singapore have tried to encourage their workers to treat the factory as a family unit. For example, on many social occasions, the management speech would begin with the phrase 'as members of one family'.

A major source of cultural influence on young women is their living away from home in urban areas where they are frequently caught in the conflict between 'the modern' and the 'traditional'. Traditional values hold that they should provide for the parental homes at the expense of the self. But in the factories there are pressures to be a 'modern girl', i.e., one who dresses fairly well, uses make-up, attends parties. From time to time, beauty shows and make-up classes are organized by the factories and hotels for the girls. In other words, with their new cash incomes the girls are encouraged to be a particular kind of consumer. The hope generated is that by looking pretty the girls may be able to attract highly paid men as husbands, and hence be assured of a fairly secure future.

In predominantly Muslim areas, these factory girls are usually 'given a bad name' with their morals and dress styles criticized by local community leaders, women's groups and welfare organizations. Many of these Muslim girls, in fact, have been reported as becoming 'misfits' when they return home to their rural community. In these communities, women are perceived as the upholders of traditional ways of life, morality and 'traditional values'. Changes in women's role and their participation in economic and social life bring about fears and anxieties. For example, young Malay women from the rural areas working in the industrial areas of Penang and Shah Alam in Malaysia have been accused of being most susceptible to 'Western' influence.

Traditionally, 'proper' Malay girls are kept under strict surveillance from puberty onwards. Images of 'proper young women' are those of shyness and bashfulness. However, with increased urbanization and exposure to education, many Malay women have refused to be governed by these images. The urban Malay women are demanding more say in the running of their own lives and greater freedom of choice. The economic support given by these young women to their parental households is a strong influence to changing parental perceptions. However, at the village and community level and even at the national level, reactions to these women have been ambivalent and contradictory.

While the young women who send remittances to the villages are seen as 'good daughters', young women in industries are also stereotyped as forgetting their culturally expected role and wasting money on expensive clothes and beauty products. In many quarters, industrial jobs are suspect as they bring young Muslim women into contact with men and are seen as environments where young women are said to undergo moral corruption. In fact, many of these women face great social difficulties when they return to the villages. The stress and conflict produced by inappropriate images may not always produce the mass hysteria that occurs from time to time among the Muslim girls working in factories, but they certainly take their toll on the emotional health of these women. In other words, modernization often introduces new role possibilities that cannot be handled by traditional perceptions of women.

Conclusion

In spite of all the conditions discussed in this section, the provision of wage employment away from home and the patriarchial family system is generally viewed by the women themselves as 'liberating'. They are granted a measure of economic independence and with it their status within the family has improved as they are no longer regarded as 'just another mouth to feed'. They have more personal freedom; they have access to a wider range of life experiences and activities. However, within the context of the industrial sector itself, they remain at the lowest rank of the hierarchy earning low wages, often working in poor working conditions with little hope of vertical mobility in terms of getting skilled industrial jobs. Although life options may have improved, in terms of working conditions, women find themselves in a highly structured environment over which they have little control. The clustering of women in particular occupations and at the bottom of the skill pyramid is the result of the interaction of socialization patterns and socio–economic discrimination. One immediate way of reducing this heavier burden that present industrialization policies have placed on women is to ensure that skill-formation and upgrading is available to women at their workplace, so that they can quickly respond and take advantage of the transition to higher technology industries. To what extent these conditions will be improved by shifting to high technology industries in countries like Singapore remains to be seen. At the moment, however, it is the migrants and local women workers who are retrenched as the result of this restructuring.

Pay and working conditions, the traditional problems around which organization and resistance occur, can for women be linked to another set of issues around gender – the problems of their personal lives, partially freed from the ties they have to their social and cultural background. In the urban areas, under the impact of industrialization, it is usually assumed that traditional perceptions of women change and with it, male – female relationships. However, even in a situation of rapid change, traditional sex-roles and perceptions may not change but instead become reintegrated into new situations. The same intricate mechanisms which link livelihood to family structure and attitudes may continue to operate even though the framework is more heterogenous and complex.

Although more and diverse life opportunities are offered to women in the urban areas, many women migrating to urban areas continue their traditional, 'female' tasks within the occupational structure of the city and workplace. Although a range of different life choices are opened up for women in the urban areas, it is usually the women with certain levels of education who are able to take advantage of these. Marriage patterns and the nature of leisure do change in the urban areas, but these changes are accompanied by strains and conflict.

Notes and References

1. Gus, E., 1982, 'Spearheads of Industrialization or Sweatshops in the Sun?' A Critical Appraisal of Labour Conditions in Asian Export Processing Zones, ILO-ARTEP, Bangkok.
    Kuwahara Yasuo, Teruo Harada and Yoshihiro Mizuno, 1979, 'Employment Effects of Foreign Direct Investment in ASEAN Countries', ILO, Geneva.
    UNIDO, 1980, 'Export Processing Zones in Developing Countries', Working Paper No. 19.
2. Barnet, R.J. and Muller, R.E., 1974, *Global Reach: The Power of Multinational Corporations*, Jonathan Cape, London.
    Sharpstone, M., 1975, 'International Sub-Contracting', in *Oxford Economic Papers*, Vol. 27, No.1
    Vittal, N., 1977, 'Export Processing Zones in Asia: Some Dimensions', Asian Productivity Organization, Tokyo.
    Datta-Chaudun, M., 1982, 'The Role of Free Trade Zones in the Creation of Employment and Industrial Growth in Malaysia', ILO-ARTEP, Bangkok.
3. *The Economist*, 1980, 6 December, London.
4. *The Economist*, 1980, 15 November, London.
5. *The Economist*, 1981, 3 January, London.
6. BBC Documentary, 'Shirts Off Our Back', London.
7. *The Far Eastern Economic Review*, 1979, 18 May, Hong Kong.
8. United Nations Committee for Trade and Development (UNCTAD), 1981, *Fibres and Textiles*, United Nations, New York.
9. Currie Jean, 1979, 'Investment: The Growing Role of Export Processing Zones', The Economist Intelligence Unit Ltd., Special Report No. 64.
    Frobel, *et al.*, 1977, *The New Internationalization of Labour*, Hamburg.
10. 'The Changing Role of South East Asian Women', 1978, *Pacific Research*, Vol. 9.
    Linda Lim, 1978, 'Women Workers in Multinational Corporations: The Case of the Electronics Industry in Singapore and Malaysia', Michigan Occasional Papers No. 9.

Elson, D. and Pearson, R., 1981, 'Internationalization of Capital and its Implications for Women in the Third World', in K. Young, *et al., Of Marriage and the Market*, CSE Books, London.

N. Heyzer, 1978, 'The Relocation of International Production and Low-Pay Women's Employment', Paper presented to the International Conference on the Continuing Subordination of Women in the Development Process, IDS, Sussex.

N. Heyzer, 1981, 'From Rural Subsistence to an Industrial Peripheral Workforce: Malaysian Female Migrants and Capital Accumulation in Singapore', in L. Beneria, (ed.), *Women and Development*, Praeger Press, U.S.A.

11. Celia Mather, 1980, 'Being Industrialized: Implications of the New Wage Labour in the Hinterland of Jakarta, Indonesia', Unpublished paper, n.d.

12. Cynthia Enloe, 1980, Sex and Levis-The International Division of Labour, government Dept., Clark University, Worchester, USA.

13. Janet W. Salaff, 1976, 'Working Daughters in the Hong Kong Chinese Family', in *Journal of Social History*.
    Janet W. Salaff and Aline Wong, 1977, 'Chinese Women at Work', in Stanley Kupinsky (ed.), *The Fertility of Working Women*, Praeger, New York.

14. C. Matther, op. cit.

15. Beck, L., and Keddie, N. (eds), 1978, *Women in the Muslim World*, Harvard University Press, Cambridge, Massachusetts.

16. Arrigo, Linda Gail, 1980, 'The Industrial Workforce of Young Women in Taiwan', *Bulletin of Concerned Asian Scholars*, Vol. 12, No. 2.
    Lydia Kung, 1978, 'Factory Women in Taiwan and Hong Kong', Paper presented at the Association for Asian Studies Meeting, Chicago.

17. Matsuo Kei, 1977, 'The Working Class in the Masan Free Export Zone' in AMPO Special Issue on *Free Trade Zones and Industrialization of Asia*, Tokyo.
    Cho Boun Jong, 1976, 'An Economic Study of the Masan Free Trade Zone', in Krueger, A.O. (ed.), *Trade and Development in Korea*, Korean Development Institute.

18. Stephen Tang, 1978, 'Dependent Development and the Reproduction of Inequality: Young Female Workers in Hong Kong'. Unpublished Paper, University of Hong Kong.
    Tse, C., 1981, *The Invisible Control*, Centre for the Progress of Peoples, Hong Kong.

19. Paglaban Enrico, 1978, 'Workers in the Export Industries: Philippines', *Pacific Research*, Vol. 9, No. 3/4.
    Robert Snow, 1977, 'Dependent Development and the New Industrial Worker: The Export Processing Zone in the Philippines', Ph.D. Dissertation, Harvard University.

CHAPTER 7

Subordination and Emancipation

From the proceding chapters, it is clear that over the last decade, women's position in society and the ways in which it is being affected by development strategies and government policies in the South-East Asian region has become an issue of clear concern to governments, international agencies and to women themselves. This is no longer a concern of a 'Western-influenced' middle class minority, but a major aspect of the 'development problem'. Increasingly, it has become the enlightened self-interest of governments to be aware of forms of women's subordination and the key issues hindering women's emancipation, taking into consideration the fact that the poorer sections of society as a whole have a very unequal access to social benefits with women having to bear the bulk of this inequality.

Subordination of Women

Various forms and bases of women's subordination continue to impede the 'integration and participation of women as equal partners'. The following section draws together these forms and bases of women's subordination as in the sectors discussed in this book.

a. *The Impact of agricultural change on women*
As has already been seen, in South-East Asia agriculture is still the major sector within which the vast majority of women find their livelihoods. Women dominate food production in household subsistence agriculture. With the introduction of changes to raise land productivity, substantive changes have occurred in the position of women with the following effects for women's subordination:

The weakening of women's authority. In household subsistence agriculture, women have considerable authority and decision-making powers by virtue of their work participation. However, with the introduction of new technology and the extension of cash crop production, the roles of women change. The household member who gains first access to the productivity package (i.e. the new technology, credit, information, bureaucratic linkage, etc.) is usually the male head of the household.

The increasing commercialization of agriculture, supported by enormous government investment in terms of systematic research and skilled personnel, has had a differential impact on men and women because women have been largely excluded. Generally, women have remained in subsistence agriculture while the men are being drawn into the technically advanced sectors. Both these factors act to the detriment of the women as their decision-making powers are weakened.

The increase in the burden of work. The marginalization of women's role also takes another form. The change in women's position as the result of agricultural changes does not necessarily mean a decrease in labour participation. Women's work usually remains 'integrated' into the agricultural system. But this integration is not central but marginal to the processes of development. When the agricultural changes involve both additional labour-intensive work and higher productivity work, it is the men who are drawn into the high productivity areas. Hence women's work-load can increase side by side with the introduction of 'improved methods'.

Limited participation in newly-formed organizations. Productivity changes also involve the creation of bureaucracies and new forms of organization. These new institutions give more prominence to men rather than women. Besides the in-built bias of these institutions, women's participation in them is hindered by their work burden. Much of women's household labour such as fetching water, fuel and general home-caring takes five to six hours and their technical base remains low because it is not profitable in monetary terms from the point of view of planners to develop improved methods in these areas of work for the rural women.

Lack of alternative central roles. Frequently, development planning has neglected to offer women alternative central roles when their traditional roles are eroded as a result of change. Recently, there have been pressures to take account in the planning process of some of the social consequences resulting from these changes. There have also been attempts to build up 'delivery or support services' to women as part of rural development. This process has brought about the arrival of health, educational and nutritional facilities. Some of these facilities, those that respond to a priority need, may, like the need for clean water, partly compensate for other adverse effects. However, in many other cases, women develop a new dependency on the agencies that deliver the resources.

b. The effect of urbanization on women

As was discussed, recently the rural–urban migration rate for women in the age-group 15–24 years in South-East Asia has increased very substantially, to the extent that there are more women than men migrating in this age-group. This is in fact a break with the traditional male-dominated migration pattern found in South-East Asia. The customary explanation for this new trend has been in terms of economic factors such as higher wages in the towns. However as seen in this book the economic factor alone does not provide an accurate picture. The new migration pattern must also be linked to the nature of changes occurring in the rural areas. The erosion of women's independent roles, the increasing bureaucratization and the increase in unremunerated hard physical labour in the rural areas are powerful reasons for migration among women, especially young women. Their migration involves a search for more favourable arrangements which they think could provide them with more personal and economic freedom.

However in the urban areas, the women are confronted by different problems:

Poor prospects of regular employment. The women who are vulnerable among the migrant groups are those without any or with little educational background. Those who were in the trading and other 'informal' sectors of the rural economy are better equipped and tend to continue with these income-generating activities in the towns. However the competition and the risks involved with these activities in the urban areas are high. Unless the women are part of an existing network, they face poor prospects of regular income and their work brings little promise of the security and advancement that they seek.

The reinforcement of sexual roles. Due to the vast income differentials in the major towns, there is a market for domestic servants and this form of employment is popular among migrant women since they are used to household chores. It solves their initial accommodation problem and may act as a stepping stone in their search for other more attractive jobs. It also provides them with a relatively 'secure' base from which to familiarize themselves with the new urban environment. However the work of domestic servants in many households is open to such severe exploitation as long hours, low pay, physical abuse, or no leave. The strong hierarchial social relationships faced by many women in these jobs may in fact reinforce the roles that these women were trying to escape from in the first place.

Contradiction and conflict in patterns of behaviour. The nature of employment open to women migrants in the urban areas very much depends on the structure of the urban economy. In a situation where many jobs offer serf-like conditions, where there are few alternative and rewarding occupations side by side with the growth of the 'entertainment sector' in the urban areas and the international traffic in women, many young women find themselves in occupations that trade in female sexuality. These occupations range from a-go-go dancing to prostitution. Many of these women see these occupations as offering better opportunities for upward mobility through the ability to attract men in secure positions, or through the opportunity for earning more money even if it means using their bodies in the distorted ways demanded by the enterprises they work for. The women in this sector face the problem of contradiction and conflict in patterns of behaviour. They are forced to learn new and often outrageous patterns of sexual behaviour and responses required by their new environment.

The common feature of the forms of employment in which women tend to concentrate in the urban 'informal' sector, from domestic service to sexual servicing, is the lack of customary forms of regulation of the working conditions, of the incomes given to the women and of exploitation in its various guises.

c. Changes in the plantation wage-sector and their impact on women

The spread of market forces, the alienation of land and the development of plantation agriculture all led to the growth of wage-labour which was exclusively male in character: for the plantations, male labour was required for the task of clearing the jungle under tough living conditions. Male migrant labour was recruited. Once certain occupations become male domains, women would not be hired so long as a ready supply of men was available. Thus when the attempt to stabilize the workforce was made through the encouragement of 'family life' on the plantations, the women on the plantations were mainly restricted to the reproductive sphere. When they participated in the production sphere, it was mainly as unpaid family help. There was no reason to employ women when men were available at low wages and their women could help without being paid. With the growth of industrial and other urban jobs, male labour became less available as men moved out to these sectors. The plantation women moved into regular wage employment on the plantation itself, sometimes even earning equal wages with the men employed. However, many forms of subordination continue to confront these women:

Isolation. When the migrant plantation labour was recruited, they were already isolated from the larger community by virtue of their ethnicity and their concentration in specific locations. As the men are slowly leaving for other jobs, the women continue in their isolation. By virtue of their illiteracy they are unable to find employment outside the estate and unable to make social contacts outside of the estate subculture. This isolation reinforces the already existing inequality between men and women, created by the different social and cultural systems operating among the workers.

Limited social advancement. Although women are being drawn as full-time wage workers into the plantation economy, they remain unimportant in the administration and power hierarchy of the estate. Neither are they relieved from their responsibility for the household as the men were when they worked as waged workers on the estate. The responsibilities for child-care and household maintenance falls to younger women—their daughters.

Struggle over cash income. Even when they are earning, the women often have to struggle over the way cash income is spent. The prevailing problem on the estates is the fight between the women and the men over the use of income on toddy, an alcoholic drink commonly consumed in the estate.

d. The impact of industrialization on women

The nature and pace of industrialization in South-East Asia has had special effects on women, especially young women in the region. With the rapid setting up of foreign labour-intensive industries that concentrate on the export of textile goods and the assembly of electronic equipment, more young women than men have been mobilized into these sorts of industries. There is considerable improvement in these workers' standard of life in terms of piped water, better access to urban facilities, and possibilities of mobility. The women's independent income often makes possible a change in the terms of their relationship with their families and communities. Women are released from many constraints that traditional communities put on their movements and activities. New relationships and contacts are also formed because of their new environment. However, different forms of subordination arise out of the nature of their integration into the industrialization process. In looking at these forms it is unproductive to ask whether these women would be better off without such employment. This employment in itself has certain elements of exploitation linked to the needs of industry, its purposes in relocation, the development strategy of South-East Asian countries in response to labour surplus, and the manipulation that firms make of women's traditional positions for their own purposes through their wage and management policies.

Wages. Women industrial workers receive lower wages than men in the same or equivalent categories. Women are also predominantly found in the lower ranks of the factory hierarchy. The ostensible justification for these differences is women's lack of training, and the assumption that women have less experience and financial needs as they are usually considered as secondary workers with incomes supplementary to those of the male members of their household. Whether or not these justifications are correct, employers benefit from women's inferior labour market position while the women themselves are prevented from the advancement which would otherwise be theirs.

Health. Many young women in industry suffer from health problems – those related to the use of chemicals in the production process; eye and muscular defects due to constant bending over microscopes hearing and dust problems resulting from the noise level and the dust level in textile factories. Dizziness and headaches are also common. Some of these health problems will remain with the young women even after they leave their jobs and their employers are in no way held responsible or accountable for them.

Lack of decision-making. Besides the low wages and the work-related hazards, another issue is the social atmosphere of the workplace. The women are subjected to close supervision by male supervisors. They have limited mobility to these ranks and their low status and positions provide them with few opportunities to develop roles that allow serious decision-making in their work environment. The models towards which women are encouraged to aspire are those based on the 'modern' women, that is one who puts emphasis on dressing up. The concept of feminity, the attraction of women to men, comes to mean pleasing male authority.

Role-Conflict. Sex discrimination, traditional values and sex-roles interact and reinforce each other at the workplace. Even when they have jobs, women are expected by society to be primarily responsible for the reproduction and care of the next generation. In this, opposing forces are clear: while the participation of women in the workplace is encouraged and may be a necessity to keep the household at a relatively comfortable standard of living, rigid sex-related responsibilities are still demanded of them by society. There is little fundamental change in sex roles within the family and little public institutional support for child care.

From all this it is clear that women's work and social positions are directed by larger structural and ideological systems and that these put definite limits on the degree of emancipation by laying down the rules by which men and women are obliged to act and to interact. These rules are usually hierarchical and related to issues of power and control. However, the real extent of women's emancipation does not depend solely on the nature of the limits created by the macro-level structures, in that the actions of women themselves have an impact on these structures. The rest of this chapter examines some forms of women's organizations and movements to investigate the extent to which these organizations can contribute to the more rapid emancipation of women.

Women's Organizations and Possibilities for Emancipation

Women's organizations, protest and the search for new ways of living are very real aspects of Asian life. As pointed out in Chapter 3, sisterhoods and women's solidarity, evolved to resist specific issues, were forms of organization used by Asian women at least 100 years ago. We need only to recall the colonial struggle to remember how recent protest movements and the will to remake social conditions of life were in the region. Yet women's struggles to remove structures of inequality and to rearrange relationships so as to increase their participation go unrecorded. This is to some extent unsurprising as the women themselves frequently remain silent. As a result many of the issues become 'private', peculiar only to certain groups when in fact many of these 'private problems' are embedded in the social positions in which these groups are located.

During the last decade, with the growth in women's consciousness, an environment has been created for a more open articulation of these issues in order to make them public so that grassroot efforts could be made visible and their impact be made greater. With pressures from women's groups, many of these issues are also being taken up at the national level with the declaration of the United Nations Decade for Women (1976–1985) which has as its main objective the 'integration and participation of women in development as equal partners'.

Some Governmental Efforts for the Advancement of Women

During the UN Women's Decade, the most significant effort of many governments in South-East Asia has been the establishment of national machineries that is the establishment of a central organization concerned with the co-ordination and implementation of whatever strategies a country has formulated for the advancement of women. Usually these national machineries are located in divisions already in existence within the government structure such as those concerned with social welfare, community development, or family planning. In some countries like the Philippines and

Indonesia, pro-government women's organizations already in existence were formed into national federations with functions that included co-ordination, advice, programming and implementation.

In assessing the effectiveness of these machineries and in identifying the factors that contributed to their successes or weaknesses, a meeting of 15 governmental and non-governmental experts from 13 Asian and Pacific Countries was of the view that:

> the setting up of national machineries could not *per se* be taken as a measure of the achievement of the Decade. In some countries, the commitment to the advancement of women could only be seen as token gestures since the national machines were not provided and had not acquired adequate resources in terms of information, funds and personnel, status or power within the governmental and political hierarchy to make any significant inroads[1].

This meeting also made the point that in many countries, the machineries did not bring women's issues within the mainstream of development, with the result that they are rendered ineffective through isolation. Another problem was the failure of machineries functioning at the national governmental level to mobilize successfully functionaries at the intermediate and local levels. Also, the nature and extent of women's participation within these machineries frequently left out important sectors of women from the decision-making process.

The rationale behind the creation of national machinery was to have better influence over policy and programme development. Yet several workshops held in the region have reported that the process of integrating 'women's issues' into development planning has been slow and national machinery ineffective.

While there has been some progress and some changes in the status and participation of women; the efforts to include women tend to remain compartmentalized and isolated from the mainstream of development itself. Many policies, programmes and institutions created for 'women' appear to have been set up as tokens for the decade and little consideration has been seriously given to the crucial linkages and relationships between women's position, their actual and potential role in society and the broader development process. Even the most sympathetic thinking on women's position still focuses on remedial action, *after* the crucial resource allocation decisions have been taken and the direction of economic development has been laid down. The potential of women to play central roles in development has not been recognized by governments and the underlying ideologies they represent. Yet, if governments want to ensure that the resources that they are spending on the objectives of national development get translated into concrete achievements, the centrality of women in the development process is already a necessity, rather than a luxury or an uneasy accommodation to sectional pressures.

In the rapidly changing societies of South-East Asia where many existing social structures are being dismantled, the exclusion of issues affecting women in national development planning must be seen within the planning process itself and the context of various, sometimes opposing, vested interests that make up the social milieu within which planning takes place. Ideally, development planning is essentially a national process which aims systematically to set out the steps to achieve sustained improvement in the quality of life for all. It not only involves an economic process which seeks to rationally allocate scarce resources for the productive purposes of society, but also involves a change of orientation of this development process to benefit the disadvantaged in society. In reality, however, it is very much a political process which involves bargaining by different interest groups in society about how the gains from development will be distributed. Hence, it is rare that the interests of women are explicitly considered in either the economic or political aspects of development planning, and the creation of national machinery has not changed this. That women's interests have been overshadowed by broader allegiances and subsumed in other interests is due to a variety of factors outside the control of national machinery. Some of these are deeply embedded in traditional attitudes and problems of social conceptualization, others relate to more recent changes in economic and social structures, while still others are the result of the dominant ideology that governs the organization and maintenance of social relationships, and of the planning process itself.

Under conditions of very rapid economic, social and cultural changes, there are groups (often religious groups) which turn to women as repositories of 'traditional attitudes and family values', which are seen as necessary for stability in times of social ambiguity and stress. In countries where the government's power is based on the support of these groups, there has been resistance to women's greater participation in society as such participation is seen to undermine and erode these traditional attitudes and values and therefore acts against the maintenance and reproduction of a certain social order. Many women themselves share these feelings and are ambivalent about changing their traditional positions and attitudes.

Even where traditional and religious values are less strong, there are conceptual problems in current thinking about 'development' and untested assumptions which guide development-planning and which can work to the detriment of women's position. The first of these are value-laden assumptions about the social responsibilities of men and women. Governments plan as though men support families when in reality it is men together with women who do so, and frequently it is the women who do so alone. Women and children are regarded by planners as dependents of men and therefore their needs are not directly reflected in development planning. Instead, their 'social problems', rather than being seen as an outcome of the wider social system, are pushed in to the realm of 'family problems' in which governments do not wish to intervene except for purposes of population control.

A closely related problem deals with the concept of work. In the analysis of work and its reward, sharp distinctions are made between the domestic and non-domestic spheres. Yet for many groups of women, the boundaries of the two spheres are not so clearly defined. For women in the subsistence sector and non-waged sectors of society, the domestic and non-domestic sphere exist as a single system and it is often difficult to separate work directed at household members and work directed at the market. For this reason, women's economic roles have been 'invisible' as women are classified as 'unpaid family workers'. Many women have not even been registered in census data and other statistics gathered on the economically active although they often are the main income earners for their households.

Associated with the above problem is the idea that women are not 'integrated' into the production process and therefore 'have no work' and need schemes to give them 'something to do'. Such schemes usually fail when subsidies are removed because they are premised on wrong assumptions. In many rural areas women participate fully in agricultural production and are central to many village processes. However they are excluded from development processes in the technical sense and when new agrarian changes are introduced by planners their central role is not recognized. They are also effectively excluded from the decision-making processes that affect both men and women in the development process.

Traditionally women have been fixed within the existing social structure as supportive and secondary personnel whose directions in life are dictated by the job and social requirements of their husbands. If development planning for women is to be effective, the planning process must be congruent with other broad changes in the social and political structures so that women can participate in their own right.

At present, women's interests are assumed to be included in the various groups that governments plan for, like farmers, indigenous businessmen, and even the poor. Yet on closer examination we find that these groups are differentiated and that the lives of the men and women within each group are structured in fundamentally different ways, with women usually located in the lower ranks of each group. While the interests of men and women should be conceptualized in a common framework for planning, differentiation must be made between their needs and interests but stressing the dependent relationships and interaction between them which after all is what makes for the maintenance of life.

The lack of concern for women at the planning stage has resulted in exacerbating several problems such as increases in work burden, more losses of existing employment, and a greater decrease in their participation as compared to men, has been demonstrated in earlier chapters. Yet it is in the enlightened self-interest of governments to be genuinely concerned with women in their development planning. The nation as a whole suffers losses when women are poorly educated, in bad health, and overworked, are barred from many activities, and are prevented from participating in decision-making. These losses may express themselves as causes and conditions of more general problems of social and economic development. Including women in development planning can increase not only women's well-being but the total human resources of the nation. Women's work is important in any attempt at human resource development.

In the final analysis, the serious consideration that must be given to women in planning for development is dependent on the political will of governments as much as on the work of national machinery. This political will is of course dependent on the nature of government, the development ideology that guides planning and the vision of the future for which the planning is directed.

Governments which are sympathetic to the interest of poor communities can potentially do much to increase the possibilities for the emancipation of women in these communities. At the very least, for the purposes of policy-formulation, rural women, especially those at the lowest strata of rural society, must be given increased support. Current development efforts even by sympathetic governments have proved deficient in their attempts to reach these women. There is now widespread agreement that if rural development is to succeed, future development policies must be designed to enable rural women to perform their traditional as well as new tasks in more productive and rewarding ways.

To achieve this, a variety of steps can be taken at the policy level. Firstly, women in farm households must be recognized as farmers in their own right and extension and other services should be designed to meet women's as well as men's needs. Also, if the woman is the head of the household as increasingly happens, she must be treated as such. Secondly, serious consideration must be given to the degree of rural women's access to certain critical elements in development such as land, water, credit, money, new knowledge and employment. These elements are fundamental in determining living conditions in rural areas. Thirdly, rural women can participate in the process of development in a productive way only if some of their drudgery and work burden is removed. In this regard, plans for the development of conventional and non-conventional energy sources for cooking as well as other purposes should be considered together with the development of improved tools, improved water supply and sanitation facilities. Fourth, women must be included in educational and training programmes and in efforts to introduce better techniques of production.

As regards poor urban women, what strategies are available to sympathetic planners to deal with the dilemmas that have been created for these women by the various social processes at play? The answer to this question is not an easy one as many of the 'economic dilemmas' are also entrenched in the broader political and ideological contexts. The obstacles facing women in the 'informal sector' are not only the lack of work alternatives, but also the fact that they are unorganized and unprotected and that attempts at organizing these workers have met with hostility and repression from governments. This category of women is not protected by any form of regulation of their working conditions, of the incomes given to them and of the nature of employer – employee relationship. Also many women are involved in what have been classified as 'illegal activities' within the informal sector.

Perhaps what planners can do is first to review trade and commercial licensing with the view to liberalize and reduce the illegality of some informal activities. Secondly, there is the need to promote small scale enterprises in goods and services for women. Thirdly, protective legislation for women in these sectors should be enacted.

The benefit of such measures to women would vary according to the nature of their work in the various sectors. Protecting self-employed women traders and liberalizing their licensing in the more viable activities would reduce the risk and severe competition that many women traders face. Protective legislation regarding terms of contact would improve the working conditions of many women. However, what can realistically take place at the level of policy for the informal sector will also depend on the constraints imposed by the style of job creation found in the formal sector, primarily on the nature of industrialization. When social benefits are introduced they are more likely to take place first in the organized sector of production, as in factories. For this reason, the women in the industrial sector may be relatively better off than workers in the less organized sectors engaged in livelihoods which are not subjected to regulation of wages, working conditions or attempts to upgrade productivity.

However, unless some pressure for regulation of abuses occurs, even in the organized sectors, be this the pressure of labour scarcity or pressure from women's groups, the conditions of employment faced by women in the early stages of industrialization are likely to be carried over even as wage-employment opportunities increase.

From research done on the newly industrializing countries (NICs) with high growth rates, it is clear that women's participation has been an integral part of the industrialization process. It is also clear, however, that at the policy level attention must be given to the nature and form of integration of these women into the labour market. Most occupations in these countries are 'sex-typed' and persons of one or other sex tend to predominate in a particular group of industries accordingly.

Sex discrimination, traditional values and sex-roles interact and reinforce each other at the workplace and women remain concentrated at the lower ranks of the job hierarchy, earning wages that are lower than men and exposed to many work hazards. Legislation if adequately enforced, can improve the working conditions of women at the workplace, and steps must be taken to convince the employers that it is in their self-interest to implement such legislation.

As increasingly the wages of men alone are insufficient to provide families with an acceptable standard of living and women are obliged to become wage earners, governments must accept a greater responsibility for the reproduction of the next generation and be prepared to establish institutional support in terms of better child care facilities. At the moment, women even when they are major wage earners bear the main responsibility for child care and family welfare.

To conclude, the essential message of this section is first that government policies must begin with the recognition that women are central to their societies, as men are, and that all development policies affect women, although often in ways different from men. Hence, knowledge about women, like accurate information about men, is an essential input to the development planning process. The data base used for planning must be differentiated by sex along with other variables.

Secondly, women must be integrated into the national developmental process in ways that both advance development and the interests of women. This form of integration is consistent with the call for a 'people-oriented approach' to development and for human resource development. It can no longer be assumed that the benefits of economic development will automatically reach women. There must be a clear understanding of women's position in society and of their importance to the development process to do this.

Finally, the efforts to include women productively in economic development should take place within a more broad-based context of changes in the social and political structure which would allow the participation of women as full and equal partners. If development strategies are to be successful, there must be a greater mobilization of women as productive agents. Their capability, motivation and resourcefulness in planning and bettering their own conditions and articulating their needs must be harnessed. At the moment, what is lacking is often not necessarily physical resources but the capacity for organization, leadership and trust – factors which can only come about through active participation and decision-making, not only at the local level but also at the top policy-making level which is still dominated by men.

Notes and References

1. Report of the Expert Group Meeting on 'Forward-Looking Strategies for the Advancement of Women', ESCAP, 1984.

CHAPTER 8

Women's Organizations and Mobilization

Non-Government Organizations and Grassroots Women's Movements

The spread of non-governmental women's organizations and grassroots women's movements over the last decade in South-East Asia is in response to a combination of factors: the lack of possibilities for emancipation within the social formation of structures that many women find themselves facing; inactivity or slowness at the governmental level in dealing with issues that affect women; the growth in awareness that women in poor communities suffer disproportionately from many 'development' processes, from the cleavages and conflicts of these communities, and from the material basis of inequality; the call by development thinkers (whether rhetoric or honest policy) for people's participation in their own development; the dissatisfaction of certain groups of women that women in poor communities have often been excluded from the many social benefits that have generally accompanied the rapid social change occurring in the region and the support for local women's organizations at the international level.

This final section of the book examines the creation of alternative organizations, and the extent to which these organizations, non-governmental organizations and grassroot groups have been successful in their attempts to mobilize and influence the lives of women with whom they work.

Women represent a category that cuts across class, ethnicity, ideological positions and identities. As a by-product of this, non-governmental organizations in South-East Asia are far from being a homogeneous group. Their characters vary in the way they approach the question of women, in their assessment of the basis of women's subordination and in the formulation of their policies for women's emancipation. Generally, in South-East Asia, leaders of contemporary women's movements are middle-class educated women. There have been attempts to experiment with inter-class philosophy and structures including alliance with women trade unionists and women workers. These experiments have shown up the need for skills to manage inevitable tensions and conflicts arising from inter-class differences. The range of women's organizations in South-East Asia includes the more cautious organizations that work within the constraints of the social and political contexts often acting as agents for the enforcement of official policy among the women they work with; professional women's groups which voice the concern of women in poor communities and organizations that question the existing discriminatory structures. The latter type try to organize women and raise their consciousness of their position, so that women in poor communities will eventually have the confidence to identify and articulate their problems and formulate their own solution.

The first type of NGOs is the most common one in Thailand, Malaysia and Indonesia. They often receive support from governments and international agencies and are engaged in income-generating projects for women in poor communities, carrying out family planning, hygiene and nutritional educational work among women, providing cooking and sewing classes and other handicraft training. Some are engaged with the organization of co-operatives and credit systems for women, literacy programmes and the creation of better water and fuel systems.

All these activities are certainly important and they have substantially improved the day-to-day life of women in the poor communities. However, seldom do they question the traditional positions of women or help in moving away from gender type training programmes. They are concerned with the provision of services rather than changing the consciousness of women. They often function without much power even within the village social system. They have difficulty sustaining the interest of many local women, except in cases where they have managed to evolve small scale rotating funds or credit systems to finance small business, handicrafts and income-generating projects among women.

The second type of NGO exists in Thailand and Malaysia and consists of the educated elite women (the professional women, for example lawyers, researchers, welfare officers, lecturers) who articulate from time to time the concerns of groups of women to increase the awareness of policy-makers and the public. In Thailand, for example, this group has frequently voiced their concern over the sexual abuse of women, the situation of women in prostitution and the conditions of child workers; also the treatment of rape victims, the chaining of some women by brothel owners especially after the Phuket fire in Thailand[1]; the involvement of some police with these owners, the abuse of children, etc. One of these groups in Thailand has set up an emergency home for women in crises. Another, after the Phuket fire, started organizing women in prostitution in Bangkok. Similarly in Malaysia, various groups of educated upper and middle-class women have organized a centre for battered wives and held an exhibition and workshops on sexual violence against women.

The work of these organizations is necessary as part of the overall consciousness-raising effort. Much of their support comes from voluntary organizations. These kinds of groups, potentially, could transform themselves into legitimate pressure groups, especially if they build up closer linkage with the women whose concerns they are expressing as well as a closer linkage with sympathetic groups involved with national policy planning and implementation. At the moment, however, they exist as small, loosely structured groups with the major part of their time concentrated on the advancement of their careers, on balancing the roles of career women, mothers and wives. Their concern for women in other communities is usually part-time concern.

In the Philippines there is currently more consciousness among educated middle-class women than in Thailand or Malaysia of the need to organize and to become a social force at national level. They have realized the importance of forming coalitions and consolidating their efforts. However, there are differences and tensions among the various groups. Some groups, said to be from the Makati-based upper and middle-class groups, see the Marcos government, especially after the assassination of the moderate opposition leader Benigno Aquino, as responsible for the mismanagement of the country's political and economic system. Their main aim is to press for the ending of the Marcos government and they have called themselves WOMB – Women for the Ouster of Marcos and Boycott.

Another coalition of women's organizations in GABRIELA – General Assembly of Women for Reforms, Integrity, Equality, Liberty and Action. They are again made up of largely middle-class/lower middle-class 'women with a more radical analysis of their country's situation. This group agrees that the Marcos government must step down but they argue that even after the government steps down, the country's problem will remain if the Filipino people do not consciously and deliberately address problems of alternative government and new directions for Filipino society.

Besides these two broad alliances, many Filipino women are also involved in multi-sectoral umbrella organizations like Coalition for the Restoration of Democracy (CORD) and the Nationalist Alliance for Justice, Freedom and Democracy (Nationalist Alliance). These two organizations are mass protest movements. The extent and impact of women's participation is still unclear and the topic is being studied.

The Philippines example is not the general trend in other South-East Asian countries although there have been some spill-over effects due to women's cross-national networks. The attempt to use drama, theatre and songs to express issues of protest, for example, is being used by some groups in Malaysia after being exposed to these forms of expression in the Philippines.

The third type of women's group found in South-East Asia give emphasis to organizing working-class women and these will be discussed in greater detail than the rest. The objectives of these groups are to get working-class women to assess critically the conditions they have taken for granted, to act upon their grievances and to develop some confidence and self-reliance. Generally, these NGOs have expressed concern over the effects of hierarchical structures, over questions of land ownership and the exercise of power as well as of various organizational constraints such as governmental interference with NGOs, the proliferation of governmental bureaucratic organizations that have resulted in confusion over directions, and of the lack of motivation on the part of personnel in these organizations to mobilize people for sustained community development.

The underlying principle of these NGOs in the effort to encourage 'people's participation in their own development' is that no long-term change is possible at the local level without changes in the structures that have ossified the society and that have created a sense of skepticism and distrust. They seek for alternative ways of organizing local communities for development, ways that seek to free the various forms of women's subordination from being interwoven into the fabric of socio-cultural formations.

The issues around which organization takes place are not merely economic or recreational ones. They work to break down the isolation of women in the village and to establish mutual multiple relationships among women across a variety of boundaries like ethnicity, class and locality, and to create an awareness of the commonality of women's situations and interests. Organizationally, these groups are loosely structured in the sense that many are not registered organizations as such. Rather, they are small groups of women, made up frequently of trusted friends. These different groups are more or less aware of one another and many exist together within networks.

The leaders of these groups are usually women from the middle-class with a certain educational level who have strongly identified with the cause of women in poor communities. In other words, the leadership of these groups usually comes from outside the community. In the initial stages, these outside leaders provide a useful role in increasing awareness and at initiating efforts at organization as frequently women in poor communities suffer from intimidation based on social, cultural and political inequality. Also their dependence on traditional structures and relationships increases their vulnerability to retaliation and repression by the interest groups they question.

The aim of some of these leaders is to eventually phase themselves out of the leadership positions as the local women become more confident in organizing themselves. Their purpose is to enable women in poor communities to grow in their capabilities to the point where they are able to work with other groups on an equal basis. This means that the women's leaders themselves have to be emotionally and mentally stable people, sensitive to the problems of others, to enable leadership to grow within the group they work with, help the group deal with its own inner conflicts and to keep the group together during periods of stress.

Some brief examples will illustrate better the working of these groups. In Malaysia, the Philippines and Thailand, small groups of educated women work with women in the squatter areas, in plantations and export-processing zones. Where possible these leaders take on jobs in community development, otherwise they work as volunteers or on action-oriented projects that are funded by various agencies, some of which are foreign-based and some funded by agencies within the United Nations.

The approach of these organizations is to help women in poor communities identify and discuss their problems, to show how their problems are linked to their social systems, and to convince them that their problems are legitimate issues for government or trade union action. This is usually done by identifying some local committed women who are or have been motivated to resolve certain pressing neighbourhood issues, e.g., problems of school drop-out rates in the rubber estates, threats of rape during working hours in the estate, conflicts over water supply (women are usually the ones who collect the water from the stand-pipes) in the squatter areas. In Bangkok, the fire in Phuket and the chaining of women in brothels aroused widespread disgust and became a controversial issue. These issues become points of mobilization as the women's leaders tried to involve local women in discussion. The local women in turn become mobilizers themselves acting as a sort of action-oriented group within their own community.

In the case of the mobilization process in the rubber estates, women leaders identified some estate women to act as 'informal leaders'. Continued discussion with these 'informal leaders' over a period of time led to the identification of a variety of problems facing women on the estate. The next step was to build an understanding of why these problems exist and what the women themselves could do about them, even in a small way.

For example, the issue of school drop-out rates among young estate women was handled in the following manner: Some of the 'informal leaders' who had a certain level of education acted as teachers in the evenings, providing tuition for children, particularly for young girls. These 'informal leaders' sought the help of some teachers in the estate schools. They also went around discussing this and other problems affecting women with other women tappers. Many of these 'informal leaders' are also members of trade unions. They do succeed from time to time in persuading these male-dominated unions to take up women's issues, for example the provision of child-care facilities for women tappers. A similar approach to action takes place in a squatter area of Malaysia where quarrels occur daily among women about water collection. In one particular squatter area, there is only one stand-pipe in the whole village with dozens of plastic tubes leading water from the pipe to the individual houses for collection. Water runs for a fixed number of hours a day. Conflict often occurs among the women of the village over the use of the pipe.

The women's leaders operating in the area held meetings first with interested women, those who brought the problem to the attention of the women's leaders, about possible solutions. These leaders, in turn, went from house to house with some relatively respected local women. This process is usually tedious and prolonged, but it allowed a working consensus to be formed among women who were hostile towards each other. Eventually all the women agreed to the drawing up of a weekly time-roster for water collection. The 'action group' with the help of the women leaders also made appeals to the local authorities to install more water pipes. Through such grassroots actions, the leaders believe that the local women will slowly come to build up their capacity for identifying common problems and acting as a group to solve them. The women's leaders believe that only in this way will village women learn the processes of decision-making, making representations and improving their social position. There is no doubt that the efforts of these women's leaders have had an effect in increasing the awareness of women in poor communities which are often neglected by the government bureaucracies.

In Thailand, after the Phuket fire, the social circumstances, public opinion and social environment were ready for the promotion of some intial degree of organization among young women in prostitution. Some NGO groups were able to identify a few women in prostitution who were willing to mobilize and activate other women in similar circumstances.

The meetings, discussions and efforts at organization give the local women the confidence to voice their opinions in the company of others. However, these sorts of groups are almost totally dependent on the personality of the women's leaders.

Success is completely tied to the rapport and trust the leaders have built up with the villagers and other local communities. This may take a while to build up. According to these leaders, the first year of their work was extremely difficult as some people saw them as 'interfering' and 'busybodies'. Only when efforts proved successful was a climate created to introduce more self-help projects and other activities, as well as to promote better organizational techniques for co-operative action. As long as the women's leaders restrict themselves to these tasks, the local authorities usually do not interfere. In some cases, however, when the women leaders become successful at mobilization, local branches of the political parties that make up the government approach them to become members as the women's success shows up, by contrast, the inefficiency and non-action of organizations that are supposed, and paid, to take care of the people's welfare. Some women's leaders spoke of the threats they received from some of the party leaders when they refused membership. Rumours, sometimes contradictory ones, were also spread about them, for example, they are out to convert the local people to a certain religion, they were communist agents, they were government spies.

Out of everyday problems, some women leaders try to start off the politicization process, acting as catalysts in making women in poor communities aware that they share the experience of subordination because of the social system they are in. These women leaders regard this as the most difficult process as sometimes the dissonance is too much to bear in an environment where governments and traditional elites are hostile to this mode of thought, where the cultural values stress loyalty to authority, where only a small section of society is involved in such reflective and analytical thinking. This politicization process, in addition, involves major internal re-socialization accompanied by psychological pressures and personal anxiety. These pressures and anxieties may appear too uncomfortable to many women, especially in situations where an alternative vision of society is unclear or too slow to attain.

Indeed, women's groups that are involved with the politicization process face greater problems than groups that are solely involved with the solution of specific problems. The former are mainly interested to develop the consciousness of working-class women about their own problems and capabilities as women, to value the work they do and to develop practice at public-speaking. This takes a long time to achieve and results are not always immediately visible, which can lead to frustration.

Relationships among the various women's groups have not been without tensions and contradictions. Potentially conflicting strategies of the different groups have not made it easy for the groups to come together. Even when objectives are similar, like intentions of promoting an inter-class movement, integrating the analysis of women's position to more general development concerns, or giving priority to the needs of working-class women, the goals are more easily stated than realized.

Antagonism among groups can be felt due to a variety of reasons. Women's leaders committed in terms of life-style and work commitment to working-class women complain that many educated middle-class women exist in two worlds and shift between them whenever convenient; they say that these women are personally ambitious, they are interested mainly in collecting data, they tend to lose touch with the 'grass-roots' and they are prone to a workstyle that does not consult or consider the 'base' and people who have spent years working with the local community before the appearance of 'feminist groups'.

The latter type of group, in turn, perceive the former type of group as lacking openness and find it difficult to understand the resentment that is expressed at their expansion into working-class areas.

Given the political history of South-East Asia, and the switching of roles by many middle-class academics, it is not difficult to understand why this resentment and caution exists. Attempts to create a 'community of women' can never be easy, especially in the early stages. Much effort will result in fragments that do not cohere. Groups have different ways of conceptualizing the human condition, and different notions of what is of value in life. In situations like the Philippines, social conditions are such that it is easier to form coalitions and networks within the country; in many other South-East Asian countries it may be necessary to have loosely structured groups working independently of one another, until differences can be respected and more trust develops.

It is important also for middle-class women to realize that the recent emphasis on the mobilization of working-class women is only one part of the whole history of women's involvement in social issues. In fact, many working-class women themselves, independently of leadership from middle-class women, have initiated and participated in social movements and protests in South-East Asia.

Women in Social Movements and Protest Action

Historically, working-class women have played important roles in the labour movement, in student movements and independent struggles of many countries. In Thailand, Singapore, the Philippines, Indonesia and Malaysia, women have been substantially involved in these movements and also in strikes and protests alongside men. However, women's public participation in almost all cases is short-term and sporadic rather than one which in the long-term becomes institutionalized so as to sustain women's participation in the shaping of new alternatives and social formations.

The reasons for this form of women's participation may perhaps be found in the sexual division of labour and the ideology which supports it. In South-East Asia, as in many other parts of the world, men are culturally seen as really being in charge of tasks associated with the public sphere and with politics and government. Women are culturally perceived as really responsible for tasks associated with the private sphere, especially of the family. In contemporary South-East Asia, this participation in the public sphere in fact means better access to income, greater personal autonomy and control over resources, alternatives in life and greater power and control. Power, status and control are acquired in the public sphere although they are not totally independent of the dynamics within the private sphere. It is also in the public sphere that bonds of solidarity are formed with others sharing similar views of the world and similar social positions and that communication and social networks are built. It is also true that the public sphere is also one where competition, tensions and conflicts can be most intense and many cultures perceive the need to 'protect' women from being exposed to these.

The picture presented above is, of course, a simplified one as the world of the family, in reality, is never fully a private one. As an example, because of social and economic discrimination in the public sphere along lines of gender, traditionally sons are considered a potentially better source of economic security and social status for families than daughters. When resources are limited, these attitudes, supported by strong social structures in the public sphere, are played out in family choices in areas of allocation and investment. Also, by way of another example, women in families are never really 'private' people. Women enter into wider networks of social relationships through which they are able to build strategies to push their interests. However, these networks are mainly used to maintain daily life on a manageable plane.

While women in poor communities may not be involved over long periods in social movements, they are quite ready to provide initiative and even be involved in confrontations and protests when their livelihood is directly threatened, particularly when linkages are developed with other groups in society. Recently (October 1983) in Bangkok, the Thai government decided to clear certain streets of small-scale traders and re-locate them in other areas. A very substantial proportion of these small-scale street traders are women as the men in this sector are usually found in small shops, work as 'took-took' and taxi drivers, or are involved in large-scale trading.

The women did not want to be re-located as the alternative sites were said to be unprofitable, being less crowded. Furthermore, the women had been trading in the area for years and had built up their own networks and symbiotic relationships. Re-location, especially to different sites, would upset all these networks. The women protested in front of Government House, with the help of some university students and staff, some concerned union officials who were former student activists and who did not feel that they need only represent their own workers (the traders are unorganized), and even some voluntary organizations like the boy scouts (their organization disclaimed any involvement, saying that their members were involved in their individual capacity). This protest took many forms: some shaved their hair and donned the white robes of Buddhist nuns, sitting in mediation; others went on all-night vigils, sleeping in front of Government House; some others even went on hunger protest. When the police were ordered in to arrest the protesters, many women entered into open conflict with them and had to be carried away physically. Eventually, their cause was taken up by some members of parliament, the arrest orders were dropped and the women were allowed to trade at their original sites.

From these examples, the efforts that women have made in developing an awareness of their world and a consciousness of their collective strength to change it may seem small and fragmented in relation to larger developmental programmes. However, these efforts have brought about meaningful changes in the lives of small communities of women who would otherwise remain ignored by development programmes. Also, women's efforts at organizing have made problematic issues that larger developmental programmes have taken for granted and which are crucial if development is genuinely concern with equity.

It is true that conflicts have arisen among women's organizations and it is important

for women to know the causes of conflict and to develop ways of conflict management. Some of these conflicts are due to different approaches and style of various
organizations, some due to emphasis on different issues and still others due to what
are commonly called 'ego-problems'. Given the heterogenity of women and their
common interest to restructure their social position, it is in fact surprising that
tensions have not taken more evident forms usually found in other kinds of
organizations.

Conclusion

Emancipation eventually will depend on the ability of women to create sufficient consciousness and strength at the international, national and local levels to introduce,
sustain and reproduce new concepts and values of human relationships, work and
alternative structures in society so that exploitative social formations, systems and
institutions of subordination can no longer exist because the social climate or culture
refuses to allow their maintenance and because there are more attractive alternatives
for living.

Because of the social cost, horrors and failures of many revolutions, most socially
conscious women are experimenting with new ways in the struggle to break down
exploitative social formations. This experiment takes place at various levels. One is at
the external level of peaceful resistance with non-compliance and rejection of
accumulation and pleasures at the expense of people; rejection of corruption in public
office; rejection of development styles that have benefited selected groups, which
have structured differential access people have to resources and opportunities, and
rejection of forms of development where the generation of wealth and services have
run countries into problems of foreign debt, foreign exchange, pollution, depletion of
natural resources and other bottlenecks. At this level, women are not alone as many
men are also involved in the same kind of struggle.

Another level is that of promoting new perspectives and values in governments,
bureaucracies, workplaces and countries in ways which allow greater equality and
more meaningful participation and decision-making by women. In this regard, at the
national level, there have been attempts to change family law, illegal practices at work
and traditional trends in education and skill-training. At the level of women themselves, some new management styles, non-hierarchical and non-authoritarian in
character, are being practised consciously by some who are exposed to the women's
movement. Many of these women are within development bureaucracies or are
leaders of new women's organizations. The family structure and child-rearing practices of several of these women have also changed in the direction of shared parent-
hood rather than motherhood, shared housekeeping and the raising of children in less
rigid sex-related roles. To what extent these trends will spill over to all sectors of the
population remains to be seen. They are still issues for struggle.

The picture of change is less optimistic at the level of women workers in poverty
groups. Capital accumulation and economic growth have been based for a long time
on women's low wages, unpaid work, long hours of work and poor working and living

conditions. Real change would require not so much an adaptation of the existing structures as a change in the structures themselves. The situation of poor and working-class women have become top priority concern of many women's groups, and poor working women themselves. The conditions for women's emancipation at this level can only be set if there is a thorough examination of how inequality is maintained and reproduced, and if there is greater consolidation on the part of women, sympathetic governments and international agencies to act on this knowledge.

One concrete way of coming closer to women's emancipation as workers is for them to know how to reap the rewards from economic growth and technological changes that are taking place in the region. Essentially this means that women must be concerned with skill development and move from being classified as unskilled/semi-skilled workers to workers classified as having sophisticated skills. This is one way in which women can improve their employment opportunities and quality of working life. The possibilities for women to do this are, of course, limited by the kind of work available to them and the social and organizational arrangements which support this development.

In the next decade, looking at the trends of technological changes in agriculture and industry that are taking place currently in Japan, the U.S.A. and Europe, there would be a demand for more highly educated, skilled, adaptable and flexible workers in South-East Asia, given the inter-relatedness of an interdependent world. Women, in order to take advantage of this change, must already be creating pressures through various women's groups, trade unions and through sympathetic government channels for an examination of the ways women workers are viewed, the ways they are classified and developed as workers, the ways they are rewarded and the ways they are retained rather than displaced during economic crises and technological changes. These pressures must be directed not only at governments but also at employers showing that at the moment the majority of women workers are still viewed and classified as unskilled/semi-skilled workers and they receive little or no training at their workplace. It is really in the interest of both employers and governments to realize that even if they treat women workers only as organizational capital, there is a need to develop new concepts and ideas of work organization and skill formation to match developments in industrial and agricultural technology.

For the future, it is necessary for women workers to move away from their traditional skills and develop in the direction of multi-skills, not only as a way to combat boredom and monotony but equally important, to increase their range of skills, flexibility and their conceptual understanding of the work process and organizational structure. This is a way of ensuring that women workers are not confined to a narrow group of skills and understanding that they become completely vulnerable to technological, social and industrial changes. Work and skill development can no longer be perceived as discrete functions but must be seen as part of an integrated human and organizational development. The social costs of an under-skilled and inexperienced workforce is high not only for the workers concerned but also for the country and the organization.

Another future trend is the development of more employment in the service sector. In fact, it looks as though the service sector is increasingly being reorganized with the introduction of computers, microelectronics and word processors. There is increasing application of new office technologies and increasing emphasis on information, data collection and processing. Different burdens and rewards are involved in all these changes or transitions. Given the traditional gender hierarchies, women are being confined to the operator status. The introduction of the word processing technology, for example, has rarely allowed women keyboard operators to expand their employment opportunities and understanding. In order for women to benefit from technological change there must simultaneously be a change in traditional organizational and administrative structures to allow women better access, control and participation. Otherwise, future developments will continue to be moulded and introduced into workplaces based on concepts and values of the past which tended to deskill and dehumanize.

Finally, emancipation in totality is a very difficult struggle in the sense that most women's energies are spent in coping or adapting to an existing system which they believe they have no power to define and no power to alter. Processes of emancipation are also processes of internal struggle in which rights and identities are refined and frameworks of action clarified. This often involves a cognitive reconstruction and is not easy to do alone without a 'support community' or network. The processes are extremely slow and results are not immediately visible. This is because most women have learned that only by internalizing and adapting to existing social structures and cultures can they survive and be accepted socially as 'normal' rather than deviant.

In the process many have lost or repressed in profound and complex ways their capacity to respond creatively to new problems. The internal struggle to revitalize human creativity, to rediscover womanhood and strength, is an important step towards emancipation. Often self-repression blocks emancipation as effectively as external pressures. Many women's organizations are aware of this and have loosely joined together in attempts at raising women's consciousness.

The task ahead is certainly to spread the ethics of care and concern. This concern entails an alternative conception or vision of what is possible in human society. It is a vision in which women and men will be treated as of equal worth; a vision in which everyone will be responded to and no one will be left to struggle at subsistence level. The implementation of this vision requires certain reordering of human activities in terms of different priorities which will often conflict with major vested interests which will act to prevent fundamental changes from taking place. The struggle is how to ensure that sensitivity and care are values that will make for the functioning of alternative organizations. Only when economic, social and political arrangements of society are no longer taken for granted and are formed according to the ethics of care, concern and sharing will there be the erosion, even if slowly, of discriminatory social formations and gender inequality.

Notes and References

1. During this fire at a seaside resort of Puket in Southern Thailand, two young women in prostitution were burned alive, unable to escape because they were chained in their rooms.

Appendix

Wage Rates — May 1975

The average price of rubber (RSS No: 1, F.O.B., Noon Buyers) for the month ended 20th April, 1975, was 56.6 cents per lb.

At the price given above, therefore, the following rates will apply for the month of May, 1975: —

1. *TAPPERS*

PRICE ZONE
55/60

   (a) The Basic Wage will be $3.20 ¢
             Price Bonus   .10 ¢ $3.30 ¢

   (b) The Incentive for High Yielding Fields for each pound above 21 pounds will be (for both ethrel and non-ethrel areas)   8 ¢ per lb.

   (c) The Incentive for Low Yielding Fields for each pound above 15 pounds will be (for both ethrel and non-ethrel areas)   10 ¢ per lb.

   (d) The rate for scrap (for non-ethrel areas) will be 5 cents a pound wet weight. The rate for scrap for ethrel areas will be 5 cents a pound wet weight for the first 15 pounds and 4 cents a pound wet weight for poundage in excess of 15 pounds.

2. *FIELD WORKERS*

   (a) Adult Able-Bodied Males
        (Basic Wage) $3.20 ¢
        Price Bonus   .10 ¢ $3.30 ¢

   (b) Adult Able-Bodied Females
        (Basic Wage) $2.75 ¢
        Price Bonus   .10 ¢ $2.85 ¢

   (c) Young Persons up to the age of 16 years
        (Basic Wage) $2.40 ¢
        Price Bonus   .10 ¢ $2.50 ¢

   (d) Non-Able-Bodied Workers
        (Basic Wage) $2.40 ¢
        Price Bonus   .10 ¢ $2.50 ¢

Wage Rates – April 1976

The average price of rubber (RSS No: 1, F.O.B., Noon Buyers) for the month ended 20th March, 1976, was 85.7 cents per lb.

At the price given above, therefore, the following rates will apply for the month of April, 1976: –

1. *TAPPERS*:   PRICE ZONE
                                                                                      85/90

    (a) The Basic Wage will be $3.20 ¢
                                 Price Bonus   .60 ¢ $3.80 ¢

    (b) The Incentive for High Yielding Fields for each pound above 21 pounds will be (for both ethrel and non-ethrel areas)   . . .   .14 ¢ per lb.

    (c) The Incentive for Low Yielding Fields for each pound above 15 pounds will be (for both ethrel and non-ethrel areas)   . . .   .16 ¢ per lb.

    (d) The rate for scrap (for non-ethrel areas) will be 8 cents a pound wet weight. The rate for scrap for ethrel areas will be 8 cents a pound wet weight for the first 15 pounds and 7 cents a pound wet weight for poundage in excess of 15 pounds.

2. *FIELD WORKERS*:

    (a) Adult Able-Bodied Males
         (Basic Wage) $3.20 ¢
         Price Bonus   .60 ¢ $3.80 ¢

    (b) Adult Able-Bodied Females
         (Basic Wage) $2.75 ¢
         Price Bonus   .60 ¢ $3.35 ¢

    (c) Young Persons up to the age of 16 years
         (Basic Wage) $2.40 ¢
         Price Bonus   .60 ¢ $3.00 ¢

    (d) Non-Able-Bodied Workers
         (Basic Wage) $2.40 ¢
         Price Bonus   .60 ¢ $3.00 ¢

Wage Rates – May 1979

The average price of rubber (RSS No: 1, F.O.B., Noon Buyers) for the month ended 20th April, 1979, was 123.7 cents per lb.

At the price given above, therefore, the following rates will apply for the month of May, 1979: –

1. *TAPPERS*:
   (a) The Basic Wage will be $3.60
           Price Bonus   1.40 $5.00

   (b) The Incentive for High Yielding Fields for each
        pound above 21 pounds will be   . . .   .14 ¢ per lb.
   (c) The Incentive for Low Yielding Fields for each
        pound above 15 pounds will be   . . .   .16 ¢ per lb.
   (d) The rate for scrap will be   . . .   .07 ¢ per lb. (wet)

2. *FIELD WORKERS*:
   (a) Adult Able-Bodied Males & Females
        Basic Wage $3.60
        Price Bonus   1.40
        Additional Payment   .30 $5.30

   (b) Young Persons up to the age of 16 years and Non-
        Able-Bodied Workers
        Basic Wage $2.70
        Price Bonus   1.40
        Additional Payment   .25 $4.35

Managers will note that the average price for the period being above the price zone 100/110 cents, tappers, field workers and other workers specified in Annexure 'C' to the Agreement shall be entitled to an additional price bonus of 40 cents. However, in the calculation of wages for tappers, Managers should use the Ready Reckoner 100/110 and add a price bonus of 40 cents.

SOURCE: Malayan Agricultural Producers Association, circulars 13/75, 8/76, 24/79.

Bibliography

Agent of the Government of India Annual Report, 1928,

F. Aguilar, 1981, *Landlessness and Hired Labour in Philippines Rice Farm*, Swansea University, College of Swansea, Centre for Development Studies, Monograph No. 14.

S. Husin Ali, 1975, *Malay Peasant Society and Leadership*, Oxford University Press, Kuala Lumpur.

G.C. Allen, and Donnithorne, A., 1957, *Western Enterprise in Indonesia and Malaya*, Macmillan, New York.

Ibrahim Amali, 1978, 'Young Women in Prostitution', Report prepared by the Jakarta Social Research Station.

Samir Amin, 1974, *Accumulation on a World Scale*, Monthly Review Press, New York.

J. Ariffin, 1980, 'Female Labour Migration to Urban-based Factories in Malaysia', unpublished Paper, University of Malaya.

Linda Arrigo, 1980, 'The Industrial Workforce of Young Women in Taiwan', *Bulletin of Concerned Asian Scholars*, Vol. 12, No. 2.

Abdullah Malim Baginda, 1978, 'A Case Study of the Role of Malaysia Rural Women in Community Life', Unpublished paper presented to the Expert Group Meeting on the 'Development of Women's Organizations in Rural Areas', Economic and Social Commission for Asia and the Pacific (ESCAP), Bangkok.

The Bangkok Post, 1982, 'Drive to Clean Up Pakistan, Prostitutes May Face Execution', 18 October p. 6.

R. Barker and R.W. Herdt, (forthcoming), *The Asian Rice Economy*, Johns Hopkins Press, U.S.A.

R.J. Barnet, and R.E. Muller, 1974, *Global Reach: The Power of Multinational Corporations*, Jonathan Cape, London.

Dean Barret, 1980, *The Girls of Thailand*, Toppan Printing Co., Hong Kong, pp. 108–13.

P.T. Bauer, 1948, *The Rubber Industry*, Harvard University Press, Cambridge.

P.T. Bauer, 1960, *Colonial Labour Policy and Administration*, London.

L. Beck, and N. Keddie, (eds), 1978, *Women in the Muslim World*, Harvard University Press, Cambridge, Massachusetts.

Willard A. Beling and George O. Totten (eds), 1970, *Developing Nations: Quest of a Model*, Van Nostrand Reinhold Company, New York.

Harry Benda, 1972, *Continuity and Change in S.E. Asia*, S.E. Asian Studies Monograph, Yale University, New Haven.

H. Benjamin and R.E.L. Masters, 1965, *Prostitution and Morality*, Souvenir Press, London.

S. Dithakar Bhakdi, 1976, 'Problems Concerning Prostitution and Trafficking in Women in

Thailand'. The National Council of Social Welfare, Thailand.

M. Bienefeld, 1975, 'The Informal Sector and Peripheral Capitalism: The Case of Tanzania', in *IDS Bulletin*, Vol. II.

Anne L. Blasing, 1982, 'Prostitution Tourism from Japan and other Asian Countries', Presented to the first Asian Consultation of Trafficking in Women, Manila.

A.H. Bose, 1974, *The Informal Sector in the Calcutta Metropolitan Economy*, ILO World Employment Programme, Geneva.

E. Boserup, 1971, *Women's Role in Economic Development*, Allen and Unwin, London.

Jan Breman, 1974, *Patronage and Exploitation*, University of California Press, Berkeley.

R. Bromley, and C. Gerry (eds), 1979, *Casual Work and Poverty in Third World Cities*, John Wiley and Sons, Chichester.

A. J. Burkart and S. Medlik, (eds), 1975, *The Management of Tourism*, Heinemann, London.

Mayra Buvinic, *et al.*, (eds) 1983, *Women and Poverty in the Third World*, Johns Hopkins University Press, London.

BBC Documentary, 'Shirts Off Our Back', London.

Cho Boun Jong, 1976, 'An Economic Study of the Masan Free Trade Zone', in Krueger, A.O. (ed.), *Trade and Development in Korea*, Korean Development Institute.

Harry Clement, 1961, *The Future of Tourism in the Pacific and the Far East*, U.S. Department of Commerce, Washington; Nat Colletta, 1977, 'Class and Cultural Mainifestations of Malay Education in a Plantation Context', in John Lent (ed.), *Cultural Pluralism in Malaysia: Polity, Military, Mass Media, Education, Religion and Social Class*, Centre for South-east Asian Studies, Northern Illinois University, Report No. 14.

William Collier, 1974, Suentoro, Gunawan and Mokali, 'Agricultural Technology and Institutional Change in Java', in *Food Research Institute Studies*, Vol. 13, No. 2, March.

William Collier, 1981, 'Agricultural Evolution in Java', in Gary E. Hansen (ed.), *Agricultural and Rural Development in Indonesia*, Westview Press, Colorado.

Sean Conway, 1980, 'Natural Rubber Gaining Ground Ahead of New Agreements', *The Times*, London, 29 September.

Lorraine Corner, 1980, 'Mobility in the Context of Traditional Family and Social Relationships: Linkages, Reciprocity and Flow of Remittance. Malaysia: Padi Villages in Kedah Muda Region', 1980 Seminar Series, Development Studies Centre.

P.P. Courtenay, 1979, 'Some Trends in the Peninsular Malaysia Plantation Sector, 1963–1973', in J. Jackson and M. Rudner (eds), *Issues in Malaysian Development*, Heinemann Educational Books, Kuala Lumpur.

E. Croll, 1978, *Feminism and Socialism in China*, Routledge and Kegan Paul, London.

Jean Currie, 1979, 'Investment: The Growing Role of Export Processing Zones', The Economist Intelligence Unit Ltd., Special Report No. 64.

Dahlan, 'Micro-Analysis of Village Communities in Peninsular Malaysia: A Study of Underdevelopment', in H.M. Dahlan (ed.), *The Nascent Malaysian Society*, Kuala Lumpur, 1976.

M. Datta-Chaudun, 1982, 'The Role of Free Trade Zones in the Creation of Employment and Industrial Growth in Malaysia', ILO-ARTEP, Bangkok.

Roslyn Dauber and Melinda L. Cains, (eds), 1981, *Women and Technological Change in Developing Countries*, Westview Press, U.S.A.

The Economist, 1980, 6, December London.

The Economist, 1980, 15, November London.

The Economist, 1981, 3, January London.

Chris Edwards, 1977, 'Rubber in the World Economy,' *Pacific Research*, Vol. III, No. 6,

September-October 1977, California.

R. Edwards, 1973, *Labour Market Segmentation*, Lexington Books, Massachusetts.

D. Elson, and Pearson, 1980, 'The Internationalisation of Capital and Its Implications for Women in the Third World', IDS Discussion Paper.

A. Emmannel, 1972, *Unequal Exchange: A Study of Imperialism of Trade*, Monthly Review Press, New York.

C. Enloe, 1980, *Sex and Levis – The International Division of Labour* government Dept., Clark University, Worcester, USA.

Paglaban Enrico, 1978, 'Workers in the Export Industries: Philippines', *Pacific Research*, Vol. 9, No. 3/4.

Economic and Social Commission for Asia and the Pacific, 1981, *Economic and Social Survey of Asia and the Pacific*.

ESCAP, Report of the Expert Group Meeting on 'Forward-Looking Strategies for the Advancement of Women', Bangkok, 1984.

M.J. Esman, 1972, *Administration and Development in Malaysia*, Cornell University Press.

Hans-Dieter Evers (ed.), 1973, *Modernization in S.E. Asia*, Oxford University Press, Singapore.

Evoita and Smith, 1979, 'The Migration of Women in the Philippines', Unpublished paper presented to the Working Group on 'Women in Cities', East-West Centre, Hawaii.

FAO, 1979, 'Migration and Rural Development', FAO Economic and Social Development Paper No. 8, Rome.

The Far Eastern Economic Review, 1979, 18 May, Hong Kong.

The Far Eastern Economic Review, 1978, 15 September, Hong Kong.

Federated Malay States, 1914, *Labour Department Annual Report*. Perak, 1914, *Labour Annual Report*.

M. Freedman, *1957, 'Chinese Family and Marriage in Singapore'*, London.

M. Freedman, *1958, Lineage Organisation in Southeastern China*, Athlone Press, London.

F. I. Frobel, Heinrichs and O. Kreye, 1977, Die Neue Internationale Arbeitsteiung (The International Division of Labour), Reinbek bei Hamburg.

Theodore D. Fuller, *et al.*, 1983, *Migration and Development in Modern Thailand*, Social Science Association of Thailand, Bangkok.

Ron O'Grady, (ed.), 1980, Third World Tourism, Christian Conference Asia, Report of a Workshop on Tourism, Manila.

E. Gus, 1982, 'Spearheads of Industrialization or Sweatshops in the Sun?' A Critical Appraisal of Labour Conditions in Asian Export Processing Zones, ILO-ARTEP, Bangkok.

G.E. Hansen, (ed.), 1981, *Agricultural and Rural Development in Indonesia*, Westview Press, Boulder, Colorado.

K. Hart, 1973, 'Informal Income Opportunities and Urban Employment in Ghana', in *Journal of Modern African Studies*, Vol. II.

Y. Hayami and M. Kikuchi, 1981, *Asian Village Economy at the Crossroads*, University of Tokyo Press, Tokyo.

R.W. Herdt and C. Capule, 1983, 'Adoption, Spread and Production Impact of Modern Rice Varieties in Asia', IRRI, Los Banos, Philippines.

N. Heyzer, 1978, 'The Relocation of International Production and Low-Pay Women's Employment', Paper presented to the International Conference on the Countinuing Subordination of Women in the Development Process, IDS, Sussex.

N. Heyzer, 1981, 'From Rural Subsistence to an Industrial Peripheral Workforce: Malaysian Female Migrants and Capital Accumulation in Singapore', in L. Beneria, (ed.), *Women and Development*, Praeger, New York.

N. Heyzer, 1983, 'The Relocation of International Production and Low-pay Female

Employment: The Case of Singapore', in Young, K., *Serving Two Masters*, Routledge and Kegan Paul, London.

Albert O. Hirschman, 1972, 'Obstacles to Development: A Classification and a Quasi-Vanishing Act', in Norman T. Uphoff and Warren F. Ilchman, *The Political Economy of Development*, University of California Press, Berkeley, pp. 55–66.

Inayatullah (ed.), *Rural Organizations and Rural Development: Some Asian Experiences*, Asian and Pacific Development Administration Centre, Kuala Lumpur, Malaysia, 1978. W. Collier, 1974, 1981, op. cit.

Institute of Development Studies, 'Subsidised Labour', in *Down to Basic Reflections on the Basic Needs Debate, IDS Bulletin*, Vol. 9, No. 4., Institute of Development Studies, University of Studies.

The Institute of Economic Affairs, 1974, *The Long Debate on Poverty*, London, Second Impression.

International Labour Office, 1972, *Employment, Incomes and Equality: A Strategy for Increasing Productive Employment in Kenya*, Geneva.

The International Rice Research Institute, 'Central Luzon Loop Survey Data for 1979', IRRI, Los Banos, Philippines.

The International Rice Research Institute, 1983, Report of 'Women in Rice Farming Systems', Philippines.

. World Employment Programme Research, Tourism and Prostitution, ISIS International Bulletin No. 13, Geneva, 1979.

J. Jackson, 1968, *Planters and Speculators*, University of Malaya Press, Kuala Lumpur.

Norman Jacobs, 1971, *Modernization Without Development: Thailand as an Asian Case Study*, Praeger, New York.

M.A. Jamilah, 1980, 'Female Labour Migration to Urban-based Factories in Malaysia and Malay Women's Participation in the Labour Force', Unpublished paper presented at the Workshop on 'Analysis of Female Migration', East-West Centre, Hawaii.

S. Jegathesan, 1977, 'The Green Revolution and the Muda Irrigation Scheme: An Analysis of its Impact on the Size Structure and Distribution of Rice Farmer Incomes', Muda Agricultural Development Authority, Monograph No. 30.

Matsuo Kei, 1977, 'The Working Class in the Masan Free Export Zone' in AMPO Special Issue on *Free Trade Zones and Industrialization of Asia*, Tokyo.

Udom Kerdpibule, 1984, 'Remittances from International Labour Migration: An Experience in Thailand', Unpublished paper presented to the Workshop on 'Remittances from International Labour Migration', Economic and Social Commission for Asia and the Pacific, Bangkok.

Kin Thisa, 1980, *Providence and Prostitution: Image and Reality for Women in Buddhist Thailand*, Change International Reports: Women and Society, Calvert's North Star Press, London, p. 14. Jane Cottingham, 1981, 'Sex Included' *Development Forum*, June.

Elizabeth King, 1976, 'Time Allocation in Philippine Rural Household', Institute of Economic Development and Research, School of Economics, University of the Philippines.

K.E. Knorr, 1945, *World Rubber and Its Regulation*, Stanford University Press, Stanford.

David C. Korten and Felipe B. Alfonso (eds), 1981, *Bureaucracy and the Poor*, Asian Institute of Management, McGraw Hill, Philippines.

Lydia Kung, 1978, 'Factory Women in Taiwan and Hong Kong', Paper presented at the Association for Asian Studies Meeting, Chicago.

Simon Smith Kuznets, 1968, *Towards a Theory of Economic Growth*, Norton, New York.

B. Lasker, 1972, *Human Bondage in South-East Asia*, Greenwood Press, Connecticut.

Eddy Lee (ed.), 1981, *Export-led Industrialization and Development*, Asian Employment Programme, International Labour Organization Bangkok.

Charlotte Lim, 1980, 'The Position of Women in Market-place Trade in a Modern City State', mimeo, Sociology Department, University of Singapore.

L. Lim, 1978, 'Women Workers and MNCs in Developing Countries: The Case of the Electronics Industry in Malaysia and Singapore', Occasional Paper No. 9, University of Michigan.

Lim Teck Ghee, 1974, 'Peasant Agriculture in Colonial Malaya: Its Development in Perak, Selangor, Negeri Sembilan and Pahang, 1874–1941', Ph. D. Thesis, ANU.

Malacca Agricultural Medical Board, 1922, *Doctors' Annual Report.*

Margo Lyon, 1970, *The Basis of Conflict in Rural Java*, Centre for South and S.E. Asian Studies, University of California, Berkeley.

Majorie Topley, 1954, 'Chinese Women's Vegetarain Houses in Singapore', *Journal of the Malayan Branch, Royal Asiatic Society*, Vol. 27, Part 1, pp. 51–67. Topley, 1954, op. cit.

Celia Mather, 1980, 'Being Industrialized: Implications of the New Wage Labour in the Hinterland of Jakarta, Indonesia', Unpublished paper, n.d.

W.E. Maxwell, 1884, 'Laws and Customs of the Malays with Reference to Land,' in *Journal of the Straits Branch*, Royal Asiatic Society, Vol. 13.

D. Mazumdar, 1975, 'The Urban Informal Sector,' World Bank Staff Working Paper No. 211, Washington D.C. See also, D. Mazumdar, 1976, 'The Urban Informal Sector,' in *World Development*, Vol. 4, pp. 655–79.

Peter Michael, 1969, *International Tourism: The Economics and Development of the International Tourist Trade, Hutchinson*, London.

Maria Mies, 1982, *The Lace Makers of Narsapur*, International Labour Office Zed Press, London.

Lennox A. Mills, 1942, *British Rule in Eastern Asia*, Oxford University Press, London.

Leopoldo Moselina, 1978, *Olongapo's R and R industry: A Sociological Analysis of Institutionalized Prositution*, Unpublished Master Thesis.

Caroline Moses, 1978, 'Informal Sector or Petty Commodity Production: Dualism or Dependence in Urban Development?', in *World Development*, Vol. 6, No. 9/10, London.

Thepanom Muangman *et al.*, 1980, Report of a study on education, attitude and work of 1,000 massage girls in Bangkok with special reference to family planning, pregnancy, abortion, veneral disease and drug addiction (unpublished paper in Thai, Bangkok).

E. Mueller, 1982, 'The Allocation of Women's Time and Its Relationship to Fertility', in R. Ander, *et al.*, (eds), *Women's Roles and Population Trends in the Third World*, ILO, Geneva.

A. McFadyean, 1945, (ed), *The History of Rubber Regulation 1934–1943*, London.

T.G. McGee, 1979, 'The Poverty Syndrome: Making Out in the S.E. Asian City', in R. Bromley and C. Gerry (eds), op. cit.

Ruth T. McVey, 1978, *Southeast Asian Transition*, Yale University Press, New Haven.

NACIWID, 1978, 'Women in Development', Plan of Action, Malaysia.

National Union of Plantation Workers, 'Commitments for the Future', Plantation Worker's House, Selangor, Malaysia (no date).

National Union of Plantation Workers, 1967, 'Collective Bargaining in the Rubber Industry', Kuala Lumpur.

New Straits Times, 1979, 25 September, Kuala Lumpur.

Lin Newman, 1982, 'Shadows of Pleasure', Presented at the First Asian Consultation on Trafficking of Women, Manila.

Frank Peacock, 1979, 'The Failure of Rural Development in Peninsular Malaysia', in J. Jackson and M. Rudner (eds), *Issues in Malaysian Development*, Heinemann Educational Books, Kuala Lumpur.

Philippines Brief Report on the Situation of Masseuse Attendants, Hostesses and Hospitality Girls in Manila, First Asian Consultation on Trafficking of Women, Manila, 12–15 March 1982.

P. Phongpaichit, 1980, 'Rural Women of Thailand: From Peasant Girls to Bangkok Maseuses', *ILO Working Paper*, WEP 10/WP 14, Geneva.

M. Piore, 1978, 'Dualism in the Labour Market', in *Revue Economique*, No. 1.

A. Portes, 1978, 'The Informal Sector and the World Economy: Notes on the Structure of Pacific Research, 'The Changing Role of South East Asian Women', 1978, *Pacific Research*, Vol. 9.

A. Portes, 1979, 'Unequal Exchange and the Urban Informal Sector', Chapter III, Unpublished Draft, IDS, Sussex.

E.K. Quizon and R.E. Evenson, 1978, 'Time Allocation and Home Production in Philippine Rural Household', Yale University.

RISDA, 1982, 'Kajian Sumbangan Kaum Wanita Kepada Pembangunan Masyarakat Pekebun Kecil Getah', Unit Penyelidikan Socio-Ekonomi, Malaysia.

B. Rogers, 1979, *The Domestication of Women: Discrimination in Developing Societies*, St. Martin's Press, New York.

Janet W. Salaff, 1976, 'Working Daughters in the Hong Kong Chinese Family', in *Journal of Social History*.

Kernial Singh Sandhu, 1969, *Indians in Malaya: Some Aspects of Their Immigration and Settlement* (1786–1957), Cambridge University Press, Cambridge.

Janet W. Salaff and Aline Wong, 1977, 'Chinese Women at Work', in Stanley Kupinsky (ed.), *The Fertility of Working Women*, Praeger, New York.

James Scott, 1972, 'The Erosion of Patron – Client Bonds and Social Change in Rural Southeast Asia', in *Journal of Asian Studies*, Vol. 32, No. 1, November, pp. 5–37.

J.C. Scott, and B. Kerkvliet, 1973, 'The Politics of Survival: Peasant Response to "Progress" in S.E. Asia', in *Journal of S.E. Asian Studies*, 4, pp. 241–68.

J.C. Scott, 1976 *The Moral Economy of the Peasant*, Yale University Press, New Haven.

Ishak Shari, *et al.*, 1978, 'Rural – Urban Dimensions of Socio-Economic Relations in Northern Peninsular Malaysia: A Report from Two Village Studies', Paper presented to the UNCRD Colloquium on 'Rural – Urban Relations', Nagoya, Japan.

Ishak Shari and K.S. Jomo 1980, 'Malaysia's Green Revolution in Rice Farming: Capital Accumulation and Technological Change in Peasant Society', Paper presented to the UNITAR Conference on Alternative Development Strategies and the Future of Asia, New Delhi.

M. Sharpstone, 1975, 'International Sub-Contracting', in *Oxford Economic Papers*, Vol. 27, No. 1

A. Siamvalla, 'An Economic Theory of Patron – Client Relationships with Some Examples from Thailand'. Unpublished paper, Thai European Seminar on 'Social Changes in Contemporary Thailand', University of Amsterdam.

J. Smith and F. Gascon, 1979, 'The Effect of the New Rice Technology on Family Labour Utilization In Laguna', IRRI, Research Paper Series No. 42, IRRI, Los Banos, Philippines.

Robert Snow, 1977, 'Dependant Development and the New Industrial Worker: The Export Processing Zone in the Philippines', Ph. D. Dissertation, Harvard University.

O. Stark, 1976, 'Rural to Urban Migration and Some Economic Issues: A Review of 1965–1975 Period', ILO Working Paper No. 38, Geneva.

Government of Sri Lanka, 1981 Statistics on Women and Development, Women's Bureau of Sri Lanka, Ministry of Plan Implementation, 15 May 1981.

Ann Stoler, 1976, 'Rice Harvesting in Kali Loro: A Study of Class and Labour Relations in Rural Java'. Paper presented to the Annual Meeting of the American Anthropological Association.

Serrewat Sudarat, 1983, 'Prostituion: Thai – European Connection', A Summary Report, World Council of Churches, Geneva, July.

Iman Sudjahn and Anidal Hasjir, 1978, 'The Role of Formal and Informal Leaders' Wives at Serpang', in *Development of Women's Organizations in Rural Areas*, ESCAP, Bangkok.

A. Suehiro, 1981, 'Land Reform in Thailand', in *Developing Economies*, Tokyo, Vol. 19, No. 4, pp. 314–47.

J.K. Sundaram, 1977, 'Class Formation in Malaya: Capital, the State the Urban Development', Ph. D. Thesis, Harvard University.

Vinson H. Sutlive, 'The Many Faces of Kumang: Iban Women in Fiction and Fact', *Sarawak Museum Journal*, Vol. XXV, No. 46, 1977.

M.C. Swift, 1965, *Malay Peasant Society in Jelebu*, Athlone Press London.

Edita Tan, 1984, 'A Study of Overseas Employment Policy and Remittances: A Case Study of the Philippines', unpublished paper presented to the Workshop on 'Remittances from International Labour Migration', ESCAP, Bangkok.

Stephen Tang, 1978, 'Dependent Development and the Reproduction of Inequality: Young Female Workers in Hong Kong'. Unpublished Paper, University of Hong Kong.

Irene Tinker and M.B. Bramsen, 1976, *Women and World Development*, Overseas Development Council, Washington, D.C.

C. Tse, 1981, *The Invisible Control*, Centre for the Progress of Peoples, Hong Kong.

UNIDO, 1980, 'Export Processing Zones in Developing Countries', Working Paper No. 19.

Unitar, 1980, Papers from the 1980 Unitar Conference on 'Alternative Development Strategies for Asia'.

United Nations Committee for Trade and Development (UNCTAD), 1981, *Fibres and Textiles*, United Nations, New York.

L.J. Unnevehr and M.C. Standford, 1983, 'Technology and the Demand for Women's

Leo Van Der Velden, 1981, 'Visitors and tourists to Thailand and their eventual demand for prositution'. Unpublished paper.

N. Vittal, 1977, 'Export Processing Zones in Asia: Some Dimensions', Asian Productivity Organization, Tokyo.

Bill Warren, 1973, 'Imperialisms and Capitalist Industrialization', in *Industrialization in the Third World*, New Left Review, No. 81, Sept – Oct., pp. 3–44.

Ursula Wasserman, 1972, 'The Challenge of Synthetics', *Journal of World Trade Law*, Vol. 6, No. 3, May – June.

Wellesley Editorial Committee (ed.), 1977, *Women and National Development: The Complexities of Change*, University of Chicago, Chicago.

Benjamin White, 1976, 'Population, Involution and Employment in Rural Java', in Gary E. Hansen (ed.), *Agricultural Development in Indonesia*, Cornell University Press.

B. White, 1976b, 'Population, Involution and Employment in Rural Java', in Gary E. Hansen (ed.), *Agricultural Development in Indonesia, Cornell University Press*.

Ben White, 1981, 'Population, Involution and Employment in Rural Java', in G. Hansen, *Agriculture and Rural Development in Java*, West View Press, Colorado.

Glen Williams and Satoto, 1980, 'Socio-Political Constraints on Primary health Care', in *Development Dialogue*, No. 1.

W. Woods, 1937, *Mui Tsai in Hong Kong and Malaya*, Colonial Office, London.

Kuwahara Yasuo, Teruo Harada and Yoshihiro Mizuno, 1979, 'Employment Effects of Foreign Direct Investment in ASEAN Countries', IILO, Geneva.

S.Y. Yoon, 1979, 'The Halfway House – MNCs. Industries, and the Asian Factory Girls', mimeo, UNAPDI, Bangkok.

Nadia Youssef, 1974, 'Women and Work in Developing Societies', Population Monograph Series No. 15, University of California.

Nadia Youssef and C.B. Hetler, 1983, 'Establishing the Economic Condition of Women-headed Households in the Third World: A New Approach', in Mayra Buvinic, *et al.*, (eds) *Women and Poverty in the Third World*, Johns Hopkins University Press, London.

Index

a-go-go dancers, 53, 55, 56, 60
age-specific labour force, 42
agency houses, 69, 76, 80, 81–82
agriculture
  migration from, 37–9, 40–41, 94, 96
  reforms, 17–33, 113–15
  subsistence, 12, 24, 71, 83
  technology, 6, 11, 18–24, 113–14, 134
  women in (role), 6–7, 12–17, 121–2
Ai Batang Dam, 30–32
alcoholism, 73, 74, 83
Aquino, Benigno, 127
ASEAN region, 13, 30
Australian Snowy Mountain Engineering Corporation, 30
authority structures, 7, 113–14
  see also social control

Bakun Dam project, 30
Bangkok, 132
  migration to, 37, 45, 47
  Phuket fire, 126, 127, 128, 129
  prostitution, 54, 58–60, 126–9
bar girls, 32, 53, 59
Barker, R., 25–6
Bhutan project, 22, 24
Bogyoke Aung San Market, 44

brothels, 56, 60, 61–2, 63, 64, 128
Bureau of Women and Minors (Manila), 54–5
bureaucracies, 26–9, 114
Burma, 17, 18

Cantonese Asam, 40, 46–7, 50
capital accumulation, *xiii*, 4, 133–4
  plantation sector, 69, 70, 80
capitalism, 4, 5, 69
Carey Island Estate, 89
cash crops, 17, 22, 30–32
caste system, 3, 69–70, 71
chemical fibre production, 96–7
child(ren)
  care, 6, 27, 28, 49, 84–5, 123
  education, 42, 87, 89, 129
  in informal sector, 4, 5, 6
  labour, 39, 44, 61, 63–4, 83, 85, 87
  prostitution, 60–64, 65
  on rubber estates, 83–9, 90
Chinese migrants, 39–40, 48, 62–3, 70, 100, 109
clothing industry, 93, 97–8, 101–4
co-operatives, 28, 126
Coalition for the Restoration of Democracy (CORD), 127
coconut estates, 77

Collier, William 20
Colombo Mission, 3
colonialism, 17, 24
  in rubber plantations, 69–75
communism, 74, 89
Community Development Programmes, 27
'Conscious Women's Movement' (AWAS), 28
cooking (for income-generation), 43–4, 47
Council for Indigenous People (MARA), 26
crèche facilities, 85
credit societies, 28, 126
crops, 11, 12
  cash, 17, 22, 30–32
  high-yielding varieties, 17, 20, 21
  see also individual crops
cultural factors, 8, 16, 28, 64–5, 115, 131–2
  emancipation and, *xiv*, 109–11, 120

debts (of estate workers), 83
decision-making, *xii*, 129–30, 133
  industrial, 117, 121
  rural, 16, 28–9, 32, 113–14
development
  informal sector, 3–6
  planning, 119–24, 133
  rural, 26–32, 121–2
  theory (1950s/1960s), 1–3

development (integration approach), *viii–ix*, 6–8, 113, 133
  government policies, 118–24
  non-governmental organizations, 28, 125–31, 132
domestic service, 62–3
  migrant workers, 37, 39–40, 43, 46–7, 49–50, 115

economic growth, 1–2, 94, 133–4
education, 100, 101, 122
  of children, 42, 87, 89, 129
  of NGO members, 126–7
  and qualifications, 6, 27, 43
  see also training
electronics industry, 45, 47, 93, 96, 100, 101, 108, 116
elite groups
  rural, 18, 20, 27, 29
  women (in NGOs), 126–7
emancipation
  area if investigation, *viii–xi*
  industrialization and, 92, 104–10
  organizations, 118–24, 133–5
employment
  conditions, 4, 47, 106–9, 122–3
  see also labour
'entertainment sector', 52–66, 115
ethnicity, 3, 68, 69–70, 116
Europe, 2, 94, 97
Evenson, R.E., 12
expenditure patterns, 105–6, 109, 110
export processing zones (EPZs), 92–6, 102, 128

factory work, 92, 104–10
  see also electronics industry; ship-building industry; textile industry

family
  labour relations, 4, 5, 21, 70–71
  in rubber estates, 70–71, 73–5, 80–83, 85
  survival networks, 48–9, 50, 132
  see also household
Farmers' Organization Authority, 27
Federal Agricultural Marketing Authority (FAMA), 26
Federal Land Consolidation and Rehabilitation Authority (FELCRA), 25
Federal Land Development Authority (FELDA), 25, 26, 27
female sexuality, trade in, 52–66, 115
fertilizers, 11, 17, 18, 22, 25, 38
food industry, 43, 44, 47, 96
formal sector, 3–4, 5
free trade zones, 92, 98–9, 100

GABRIELA, 127
garment industry, 93, 97–8, 101–3, 104
German Agency for Technical Co-operation Limited, 30
girls (in prostitution), 60–64, 65–6
  see also children
government policies
  emancipation strategies, *viii*, 118–24
  rural areas, 26–9
Grace Hotel, Bangkok, 59
Green Revolution, 25

Hart, Keith, 3
health and safety (industrial), 106–7, 117
Herdt, R.W., 25–6
Hinduism, 73
homeworking, 36, 44–6, 98, 101–2

homosexuality, 56, 60, 64
Hong Kong, 94, 97, 98, 106–8
hospitality industry, 54–6, 58, 64
hours of work, 6, 12, 106, 107
household
  heads of (women), 6–7, 40–41, 122
  integration (plantation), 80–83
  in longhouses, 30–32
  rural, 12–15
housing, 31, 71, 75, 82–3, 85, 89
hydro-electric dams, 30–32

Iban society, 30–32
ILO-WEP, 3
import restrictions, 97
income
  generation, 36, 43–9, 115, 126
  handling, 13 *bis*, 14–15, 116
  see also wages
India, 61, 97
  plantation workers from, 69–74, 116
Indonesia, 7, 49, 68, 101, 126, 131
  rural change, 18–24, 28–9
industrialization, 1, 11, 17–18, 25
  EPZs, 92–6, 102, 128
  impact (on women), 116–18, 122–3
  textiles, 92–111
inequality, sexual, 3, 7, 8, 48, 116
  see also subordination
informal sector, 3–6, 100, 122
  non-wage sector, 43–50
  prostitution, *see* prostitution
inheritance rights, *xi*, 16–17, 24, 39
integration approach, *viii–ix*, 80–83
International Labour Office, 3
International Rice Research Institute

Index

(IRRI), 25
irrigation, 17, 18, 25

Jakarta, 101, 105, 106-7
Jakarta Social Science
    Research Training
    Station, 62
Japan, 2, 60, 93, 104
Java study, 12
Jogdjakarta study, 44
Jurong study, 99-100

Kali Loro study, 20-21
Kampuchea, 17-18
Kangany System, 70, 71,
    73, 87
Kedah, 25
KEMAS, 27
Kenyan Mission, 3
Kenyan Report (1972), 3-4
King, Elizabeth, 12
Korea, 94, 97, 106-8
Kramat Tunggak study, 62

labour
    absorption, 4, 41-3
    exchange systems, 15
    -intensive industries, 37,
        42, 47, 92-4, 96-8,
        104, 109, 114, 116-17
    market, 4, 5-6, 123
    migrant, see migration
    plantation workforce,
        69-70, 76-80
    relations (family), 4, 5,
        21, 70-71
Lampang case study, 13-15
land ownership, 7, 13
    access changes, 16-17,
        24-5, 30-31
    Iban society, 30-32
    migration and, 37, 38, 39
Laos, 17-18
leaders, women as, 27, 29,
    129-30, 133

McGee, T.G., 5
Madrasi, 70
Malaya, 62-3
    plantation sector, 69-76
Malayan Agricultural
    Producers
    Association, 79-80,
    136-8
Malayan Planting
    Industries'

Employers'
    Association, 78-9
Malaysia, 7, 37, 47, 48, 131
    plantation sector, 68-89
    rural change, 16-18, 24-5,
        26-8, 29-32
    textile indust ry, 98-101,
        105, 106
Malaysian Women's
    Movement, 28
malnutrition, 13, 61
Manila, 54-6, 58-9, 64
manufacturing, see
    industrialization
MAPA, 79, 80
Marcos government, 127
marketing, 36, 43-4, 122
masseuses, 37, 53-60,
    passim
men (migration), 13, 14, 37,
    40-41
middle class women (in
    NGOs), 127, 128,
    130-31
middlemen (penebas), 20
migration and migrants, 7,
    25
    in plantations, 69-74
        passim, 116
    in shipbuilding, 103-4
    in textiles, 92, 94, 96, 100
    women, 36-41, 50, 92,
        94, 96, 114-15
    women (types of work),
        41-9
military bases, 59
Minangkabau, 16
missionary groups, 28
MNC models, 1
mobilization process, 123,
    125, 128-30, 131-5
Muangman, T., 54
Mui Tsai system, 62-3
Multi-Fibre Agreement
    (1973), 97
Muslims, 16-17, 100, 105,
    109-10

National Advisory Council
    on the Integration of
    Women in
    Development, 27
National Council of Social
    Welfare, 61-2
National Union of
    Plantation Workers,

79, 80
nationalism, 74, 127
Negri Sembilan, 16
networks
    rural community, 15-16,
        18
    women's, 48-9, 50, 132
    see also non-
        governmental
        organizations
New Block Planting
    Scheme, 76
newly industrialized
    countries, 97, 123
non-governmental
    organizations
    (NGOs), 28, 125-31
    passim

'obstacles to development',
    2, 26
office technologies, 135
oil palm estates, 77-8, 80,
    81, 89
Olongapo City study, 59
OPEC, 96
Organization for Women
    Rubber Smallholders,
    28
out-work, 36, 44-6, 98,
    101-2

Pakistan, 59, 65
Palagus Dam project, 30
palm oil, 77-8, 80, 81, 89
participation
    bureaucracies and, 26-9,
        114
    development planning
        and, 119-24
    in NGOs, 28, 125-31
    in social movements,
        125, 131-3
    see also decision-making
Patpong I and II, 60
patriarchal family system,
    109, 110
patronage system, 16, 18,
    48, 49, 50
Pelagus project, 30
petty commodity
    production, 4-5
Philippines, 7, 12, 37, 59,
    68
    NGOs, 127, 128, 131
    rural change, 17-18,

25–6, 28
textile industry, 102, 107, 108
Phongpaichit, Pasuk, 58
Phuket fire, 126, 127, 128, 129
pimps, 57, 59, 62, 64, 65, 66
pineapple estates, 77
plantation sector, 24, 94, 116, 128–9
case study, 80–89
colonial period, 69–75
present-day, 68, 75–80, 89–90
politics, women's role, 28, 130
Pondok Jagung study, 29
poverty
economic growth and, 1–2, 94, 133–4
informal sector and, 3–6, 43–50
prostitution and, 61–5 *passim*
on rubber estates, 79–80, 83, 89
rural, 12–13, 17, 37, 94, 96
production, 4–5, 36, 38–9, 42, 121
agricultural, 11–12, 25–6, 122
labour-intensive, *see* labour
professional women (in NGOs), 126–7
prostitution, 32, 53, 55–6, 115
in Bangkok, 37, 54, 58–60, 126–9
social context, 63–5
vulnerable groups, 57–8, 61–6

Quizon, E.K., 12

Rawabuntu study, 29
recruitment, shipbuilding, 103–4
recruitment, textile industry, 98–102
redundancies (rubber estates), 79, 82–3, 87
relocation (textiles), 92–6
implications for women, 104–10

reasons for, 98–103, 117
resource allocation, 2–3, 119–20
rural households, 12–13, 14
result system, 72
retrenchment (rubber estates), 79, 82–3, 87
rice farming, 13–14, 19–23
MV adoption, 25–6
in Sarawak, 30, 31
role conflict, 8, 28, 64–5, 115, 117–18
emancipation and, 109–11, 120, 131, 3
patronage system, 16, 18, 48, 49, 50
rubber industry, 27–8
estates, *see* plantation sector
natural (NR), 68, 69, 73, 75–6
synthetic (SR), 69, 75–6
wages, 136–8
Rubber Industry Smallholders' Development Authority, 27–8
Rubber Research Institute of Malaysia, 74, 76
rural
change, 17–33, 113–15
community, 15–17
development, 26–32, 121–2
elite, 18, 20, 27, 29
households, 6–7, 12–15, 40–41, 122
-urban migration, 36–41, 92, 94, 96, 114–15
Rural Industrial Development Authority, 26

Sama Consortium, 30
Sarawak Dam project, 29–32
secret societies, 48, 63
Selangor estate study, 80–89
self-employment, 3, 45, 122
Seoul (textile industry), 106, 107
service sector, 43, 134–5
see also domestic service;

sexual services; tourism
sexual division of labour, 21, 38, 131
in income generation, 43–50, 115
in industry, 102–3, 123
in plantations, 71–2, 80–81, 85, 87, 89–90
sexual inequality, 3, 7, 8, 48, 116
see also subordination
sexual services, 52–66, 115
see also prostitution
shipbuilding industry, 103–4
Sime Darby, 76
Singapore, 62, 63, 131
migration to, 40, 46–7, 48
shipbuilding industry, 103–4
textile industry, 99–102, 105–9
skills, *see* training
small-scale business, 3–6, 36, 43–4, 122, 132
social
behaviour, emancipation and, 109–11
consequences (rural development), 29–32
context (of prostitution), 63–5
division of labour, 80–81
movements (women's role), 131–3
social class, 3, 37, 68
middle class women, 127, 128, 130–31
working class women, 74, 127–31, 134
see also caste system
social control, 100, 101, 104, 108, 109
social hierarchies, 3, 68, 69–71, 116
social relations
of gender, 39–40, 100–101, 104, 108–9
networks, 15–16, 18, 48–50, 132
squatters, 83, 128, 129
Sri Lanka, 54, 56
Stoler, Ann, 20–21
Straits Settlements, 70

Index

subordination, 113–18
  area of investigation,
    viii–xi
  patronage system, 16, 18,
    48, 49, 50
  on rubber estates, 87, 89
  see also emancipation
subsistence agriculture, 12,
  24, 71, 83
synthetic fibres, 96–7

Taiwan, 94, 97, 106
Tamil workers, 68, 70
task differentiation, 80–81
task system, 72, 79–80, 108
tea estates, 77
technology, 1, 2, 7, 135
  agricultural, see
    agriculture
  rubber, 68, 69, 75–6
  textile, 94, 96, 97, 106,
    110
Tennmaran Estate, 89
textile cloth production,
  97, 98–101
textile industry
  (relocation), 47
  emancipation in, 194–11
  employment/
    recruitment, 98–103
  EPZs, 92–6, 102, 128
  structure, 96–103, 104
  wages, 42, 94, 98, 104–6,
    117
Thailand, 17–18, 28, 102,
  131, 132
  masseuse income study,
    57–8
  migration, 7, 36–7,
    40–41, 45, 49
  NGOs, 126–7, 129
  prostitution, 53, 54, 59,

61–2
Third Malaysia Plan 1976–
  80, 79
Third World, 1, 3–6, 41–2,
  93–4, 96–7
time allocation survey, 6,
  12
tourism, 32, 52–3, 54, 59,
  60
trade unions, 6, 41–2, 108,
  125
  plantation sector, 74–5,
    79, 90, 129
trading, 36, 43–4, 49, 115,
  122, 132
training, 41–2, 45–7, 49,
  122, 126, 134
  rural, 15, 27–8, 32–3
  textile industry,
    100–103, 104

under-employment, 3, 4, 5
unemployment, 3, 37–8,
  108–9
  plantation sector, 73–4,
    79
United Nations, viii, 60, 61,
  128
  Women's Decade, 27,
    118
United States, 1–2, 93, 97
urbanization, 11, 18
  and migration, 36–41,
    92, 94, 96, 114

Vietnam, 17–18
village communities, 15
voluntary organizations,
  28, 126–7

wages
  informal sector, 3–6

and non wage sector,
  43–50
plantation, 71–4, 78–81,
  87, 89, 116, 136–8
textile, 42, 94, 98,
  104–6, 117
see also income
White, Benjamin, 12
women
  development roles, see
  development
    (integration approach)
  heads of household, 6–7,
    40–41, 122
  organizations, 28, 48–9,
    118–31, 135
  social movements, 125,
    131–3
Women for the Ouster of
  Marcos and Boycott
  (WOMB), 127
Women's Bureau of Sri
  Lanka, 56
Women's Section of the
  Pan-Malayan
  Islamic Party, 28
Women's Section of the
  United Malay
    National
  Organization, 28
working class, 74, 127–31,
  134
World Bank, 4
world market factories, 42,
  92–3

youth organizations, 27